MONEY TALKS

BUT WHAT IS IT REALLY SAYING?

O.S. HAWKINS

Money talks…but what is it really saying?

© 1999 O.S. Hawkins

A Publication of the Annuity Board of the Southern Baptist Convention

Unless otherwise indicated,
Scripture taken from The Believers Study Bible,
The Holy Bible, New King James Version
Copyright © 1991 by the Criswell Center for Biblical Studies

ISBN 0-9671584-1-9
1. STEWARDSHIP
248.6 – dc21

Printed in the United States of America

ANNUITY BOARD
OF THE SOUTHERN
BAPTIST CONVENTION

Dedicated to

Gene Smyers

He was there the morning I was saved and has taught me more than I could ever say with words. I have not made a major decision in life without seeking his wise counsel. This faithful steward of his own resources and also of the gospel is truly a friend who "sticks closer than a brother."

Table of Contents

Introduction

Many of us have profited by reading the biographies of great men and women of history. Suppose you were given the assignment to write the biography of an individual you had never met. Your assignment entails researching the individual's life, gathering all sorts of materials, interviewing various people who knew the individual, examining family genealogies and the like. But just suppose in your assignment that you were restricted to only one area of information from the person's life in order to write the biography. What would you request? A family history? A family tree? I once heard someone answer this question by stating, "If I were limited to one area of information in writing the biography I would ask for the individual's check book!" Our canceled checks do indeed give access to every part of our life and speak volumes about what we really think is important in life. Yes, money does talk!

As I type these words I am aware that writing about money is a sensitive subject. There is a particular brokerage firm who made quite a name for itself by an advertising campaign that suggested when they talk "everybody listens." Why, then, when the minister talks about money does everyone tune him out? The Bible has a better stewardship plan for our lives than all the Wall Street brokerage houses combined.

Some say, "Well, if money talks, it doesn't have much to say to me." Others say, "If money talks as some folks tell, to most of us it says farewell!" But our money is so much a reflection of what is on the inside of us that our Lord Jesus spoke often on the subject. Over one-third of his thirty-eight parables deal with the way we handle our possessions. One out of every six verses in the gospels of Matthew, Mark, and Luke discuss the proper use of material goods. The Lord Jesus says the way we get, guard, and give our money is a good indicator of our own spiritual progress.

As we journey together from chapter to chapter of this volume we will continue to hear our Lord affirm the fact that money talks and says a lot about what each of us think is really on the top of life's priority lists. What about your cancelled checks? What are they saying about what is truly important in your life? Yes, *money talks...but what is it really saying* about how much is enough?

Chapter One

Setting the stewardship standard

Proverbs 3:9-10

There are many pastors and churches that avoid the subject of stewardship like a plague. In fact, many modern church gurus are telling pastors across the country not to talk about money or stewardship. I find that to be very strange since our Lord spoke of it in one-third of His parables. In the churches I was privileged to pastor, we made no apologies in challenging one another in the realm of stewardship for it was a great part of our own spiritual development and growth.

Money consumes us in our current culture. Our churches are full of financial planners, bankers, stockbrokers, money managers, venture capitalists, CPAs, lawyers, and all kinds of men and women who are constantly giving financial counsel. How would you like the free counsel of a man recognized the world over as one of the richest, most successful, and wisest men who ever lived? This particular man "wrote the book" on international commerce. In fact, of him it was said, "God gave (him) wisdom and exceedingly great understanding, and largeness of heart like the sand on the seashore. Thus (his) wisdom excelled the wisdom of all the men of the East and all the wisdom of Egypt. For he was wiser than all men — than Ethan the Ezrahite, and Heman, Chalcol, and Darda, the sons of Mahol; and his fame was in all the surrounding nations. He spoke three thousand proverbs, and his songs were one thousand and five" (I Kings 4:29-32). His name? Solomon. Listen to his counsel on money management. "Honor the Lord with your possessions, and with the firstfruits of all your increase; so your barns will be filled with plenty, and your vats will overflow with new wine" (Prov. 3:9-10).

As far-fetched as it might seem, our finances generally mark the position of our own spiritual pilgrimage. We are no farther along in our walk with the Lord than the point in which we learn to trust Him with the tithe.

There are a lot of questions regarding stewardship. How can we afford to return one-tenth of our income back to God? How much should we give? There are four questions every believer should ask about stewardship: (1) What is the purpose of my stewardship? (2) What is the product of my stewardship? (3) What is the priority of my stewardship? (4) What is the promise of my stewardship?

What is the purpose of my stewardship?

 "Honor the Lord…"
Proverbs 3:9-10

What is the purpose when we attend a worship service and the offering plate is passed and we place our gift in it? Note the first three words of our text — "Honor the Lord." This should be our single most important goal in life — to honor God. It is always a good thing to check our motivation, our purpose regarding the issues of life. Honoring God should be our primary motive in everything we do, whether in our marriage, our social life, our business, or whatever.

What is the purpose of our stewardship? Some are motivated by guilt. That is, they give because they think they ought to. Others are grudge givers. That is, they give because they think they have to. The New Testament teaches us to be grace givers — we give out of a heart of gratitude and love because we want to!

The Hebrew word that we translate into our English word "honor" is very enlightening at this point. What does it mean when we are exhorted to "honor God?" Often this word is used to describe the concept of being weighted down. For example, a king is weighted down with all the accessories of royalty — the crown, the robe, the train, the scepter, the medallion. When we honor God it means that we weigh Him down. Crown Him Lord! It is closely akin to what young people used to say, "That's heavy!" This being translated means, "That is incomprehensible, awesome, powerful." To say that we honor

God means that we give Him His rightful place in our lives. He is Lord!

What is the purpose of our stewardship? Is it some lucky rabbit's foot? Is it that I give so that I might get, as some teach? Is it some legalistic Old Testament discipline that keeps me bound to the law? Our purpose in stewardship has to do with honoring God by exhibiting trust in Him.

We are nothing more than stewards passing through this world. Fifty years from now everything you own will be in someone else's name. Fifty years ago what is in your name today was in someone else's; your land, your home, your assets. When you entered this world, you entered it naked without a dime, and you will leave it the same way. In reality, we do not own a thing. We are simply stewards. Therefore, it is imperative that we honor God with our possessions. This is our purpose in stewardship. God makes an incredible statement in I Samuel 2:30 when He says "those who honor Me I will honor." What is the purpose of our stewardship? It is to honor God!

What is the product of my stewardship?

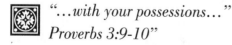
"...with your possessions..."
Proverbs 3:9-10"

We are to honor God. With what? Our possessions, our money, our wealth. Note the product of our stewardship is not just our time. It is not simply our talents. This is not what Solomon is saying. It is our treasure that is specifically addressed here. Some of us live as if our lives were a hotel corridor with room after room. As God walks down the hall, He sees the family room with the door open for Him to come in. He sees our social room, our work room, our exercise room, our activity room, our hobby room, and they are all open to Him. But in many lives when it comes to the room where we have our possessions, our money, He sees a "Do Not Disturb" sign on that door. What is the one thing that is prone to dominate and dictate our lives? Money! In fact, God says in I Timothy 6:10 that "the love of money is a root of all kinds of evil." We get trapped by government policies and our own lifestyles into thinking that money is the answer to every problem. How many times have we asked someone how they were doing, only to have heard the reply that everything was okay and they had no problems that money would not solve! Thus, the Lord indicates an area of our lives which tells us more about our spiritual condition than any other. He says it is our possessions, and hence Solomon says, "Honor God with your possessions."

It is good to have things that money can buy. However, there is something better. It is to have what money cannot buy. We have recently had another first in our family. Our oldest daughter, Wendy, is now wearing a wedding ring. As I write these words I am thinking back to the ring I gave her mom. It is now in a stickpin. I was a student in 1970 and could only afford a small ring. I remember the salesman making a special deal on the particular ring I purchased because if you look closely enough you will see a big carbon spot in the middle of it. I would be embarrassed for her to know how little I paid for it. However, that ring symbolized a tremendous amount of love as well as the confidence that God had brought us together. At about the same time a college friend gave his fiancé one of the biggest, most beautiful diamond rings I have ever seen, worth thousands of dollars. The tragedy is that their marriage did not last a year. Money can buy a lot of things. It can buy million dollar houses, but all the money in the world cannot transform a house into a home. What is really important is not what money can buy, but what it cannot buy.

While some of us desire to honor God with our lives we never think of honoring Him with our possessions. How do we do this? There are three ways in which we honor God with our possessions. First, we honor God with how we *get* it. Some people get wealth in ways that are dishonoring to God.

We also can honor or dishonor God by the way we *guard* it. The Lord Jesus said in Matthew 6:19, "Do not lay up for yourselves treasures on earth." Many guard their wealth. Some even make arrangements to keep it hoarded and guarded even after they are gone. It is no accident that our last will is called our Last Will and Testament, or Testimony. It is the last opportunity we have to give our testimony to the world of what was really important to us. One day someone will read it and tell what really held your heart because Jesus said, "Where your treasure is, there your heart will be also" (Matt. 6:21).

James spoke of a man who "hoarded" his wealth (James 5:3). In Chapter Four we will see that guarded wealth brings no joy. Some people get their stock portfolios or checking and savings statements each month. No matter how much we have we wish it were just a little bit more. When we begin to love money, it ceases to bless us and begins to curse us. No wonder Solomon said, "Honor the Lord with your possessions."

God is as concerned with how we guard our wealth as He is with how we get it. Susie and I do not have much of an estate after one-quarter century of marriage. We have invested in the bank of heaven. Much of the savings of our first twenty years of marriage is in the auditorium in Fort Lauderdale, Florida, where hundreds of people came to know Christ every year and from where dozens of missionaries have been sent. Our daughters know they are not going to get much from us. I intend to leave them something far more important than a pile of money to hoard or to guard or even to throw away. We have sought to teach them the importance of laying up treasures in heaven. Why? Because our heart always follows our treasure (Matt. 6:21). If we wait until we feel like giving, we will never do it. The natural man wants to guard it. Thus Solomon gives us wise counsel when he says we are to "Honor God with our possessions."

We honor God by not only how we get and guard our money, but also with how we give it. We are stewards of God's blessing. How we give is vitally important. The Lord Jesus still sits over the treasuries to see how His people give. One day I will stand before this great God. He is not going to say to me, "Let me see your Bible." Quite frankly there is not a page in my Bible that is not marked and filled with notations.

He is not going to look at me and ask, "Is your Bible all marked?" He is not going to say, "Let me see your sermon notebook. Are there any notes there?" I don't believe He is even going to ask for my prayer journal. Some of us may be shocked. I think He might say, "Let me see your checkbook, I want to look at your cancelled checks." Why? Because how we use what He gives us tells us where our heart is. He said, "Where your treasure is, there your heart will be also" (Matt. 6:21).

This is the purpose and product of our stewardship. The way we handle our possessions is so much a reflection of what is on the inside of us that our Lord Jesus Christ addressed it in one out of three of His recorded sermons and His parables.

What is the priority of my stewardship?

 "...with the firstfruits of all your increase..."
Proverbs 3:9-10

Note that Solomon is specific with the portion of our possessions with which we are to honor God. He calls it the "firstfruits." The Israelites brought the firstfruits of all their crops to God in order to acknowledge that He was the ultimate owner of the land. God said, "The land shall not be sold permanently, for the land is Mine; for you are strangers and sojourners with Me." (Lev. 25:23). God owns the land of Israel today, and by His grace Israel is His tenant. Thus as they brought the firstfruits offerings they were honoring Yahweh. Should we do less?

The first portion of everything we own should be set aside for God's use. The Old and the New Testament both refer to it as the tithe — one-tenth of our income. The New Testament pattern is characterized by freedom. But freedom does not negate the validity of the tithe. The *Believer's Study Bible* note says, "Tithing is only the beginning place of Christian stewardship, not the end. God does not want you to give less than a tithe, but He may want you to give so much more through His enabling grace." For me personally, I have never felt that in this dispensation of grace that I should give less than the Jews gave under the dispensation of the law. Hence, tithing is only the beginning place, the firstfruits.

In his own inimitable way, Dr. W. A. Criswell frames this point with these words, "Four hundred years before the law was given, Father Abraham paid tithes to Melchizedek, priest to the most high God. Tithing was the foundation of supportive worship of the Israelites throughout the dispensation of the law. It was in that era that the Lord Jesus lived and had His being. It was He who said we ought to tithe (Matt. 23:23). In this dispensation in which you and I live, it is the Lord Jesus Christ who receives our tithes even though our human hands take it up in the congregation. Hebrews 7:8 says, 'Here mortal men receive tithes, but there He receives them, of whom it is witnessed that he lives.' There is a sense in which every time we receive an offering in church although mortal men are serving as ushers to receive the gifts, it is the Lord Jesus Christ Himself who is receiving them."

What is the priority of our stewardship? We are to honor God. With what? Our wealth. And what part of it? Firstfruits. I well remember the day my pastor, W. Fred Swank, taught me this truth. I was a student at Southwestern Seminary and serving as assistant pastor at Sagamore Hill Baptist Church in Fort Worth, Texas. I was about to be married, and Dr. Swank called me into his office on a particular day. He was known for always being blunt and to the point. He said, "Son, your giving has been a bit sporadic." With those words I knew I was about to learn a lesson. Those of us who were "his boys" never got away with anything! I quickly replied, "Preacher, I am trying to tithe, but I get to the end of the month, and it just seems like there is not enough there." He looked at me and said, "We are to honor God with our possessions, with the firstfruits of all our increase." He continued, "Now, let me see your checkbook." Reluctantly I handed it to him. He asked another question, "What is fruit?" "That which you earn," I quickly replied. He countered, "What does *first* mean?" "First means first, the front of the line!" "Then, when you deposit your check on the first and fifteenth of each month make sure from now on the first check you write is the Lord's tithe, the firstfruits of all your increase," he said. He went on to explain to me that giving is an act of faith and showed me the meaning of Proverbs 3:5-6 which says we are to "trust the Lord with all of our hearts and lean not unto our own understanding. In all our ways acknowledge Him and He will direct our paths."

Since that day years ago I have never deposited a paycheck except that the first check I wrote after it was "unto the Lord," the firstfruit. Many years ago, Susie and I discovered the joy of giving way over the tithe every year of our married life. We did it when we had little or nothing. We did it when we were struggling with a young family. And now when we are responsible for college tuition, graduate school tuition, and weddings, we still are blessed by it. It is the priority of our stewardship.

I am often asked by people who are contemplating becoming tithers if the tithe is to be given before or after taxes. For me, I never even considered the fact that taxes to a human government should be the firstfruits. To me the issue is plain. Solomon said, "Firstfruits" — of what? "All your increase." That is how we honor God. This is the priority of our stewardship. If we wait until we think we can afford it and continue to give our firstfruits to ourselves, or to others, or to our own pleasures, it won't happen. An unknown poet framed it best when he or she said,

The groom bent with age leaned over his cane
his steps uncertain needed guiding,
while down the church aisle
with a warm toothless smile
the bride in a wheelchair came riding.
Who is this elderly couple thus wed?
We've learned when we quickly explored it,
that this is that rare most conservative pair
who waited till they could afford it!

Our purpose in life is to honor God. With what? With our possessions. And what part of our possessions? The "firstfruits" of all our possessions. There is one other question of stewardship that all of us should be asking:

What is the promise of my stewardship?

 "...so that your barns may be filled and your vats overflow with new wine." Proverbs 3:9-10

Full and overflowing! This is a far cry from the haunting call of many today — "Not enough." Here we see the John 6 principle in action. The boy gave his little lunch of loaves and fish. Thousands of people were fed and twelve baskets remained. In the words of Solomon, *"Your barns will be filled with plenty and your vats will overflow with new wine."* This is an amazing thought we find in Proverbs 3:10, "So your barns will be filled with plenty, and your vats will overflow with new wine." It is supernatural. I don't know how it works; I just know that after doing it every week for over a quarter of a century it does work. In fact, the word "be filled" in verse 10 is in the imperfect tense. It is an ongoing process. It just continues to be true as I continue to honor God with my possessions, with the firstfruits of all my increase. He just keeps on and on filling my barns.

Have you noticed that when God addresses our steward-ship in the Bible, His emphasis is not on our giving, but on our receiving? Malachi says, "'Bring all the tithes into the storehouse, that there may be food in My house, and try Me now in this,' says the Lord of hosts, 'If I will not open for you the windows of heaven and pour out for you such a blessing that there will not be room enough to receive it'" (Mal. 3:10). The emphasis is on our receiving. In Proverbs 3:9-10 once again the emphasis is not on our giving as much as it is on our barns being filled — our receiving. In the New Testament, Jesus said it like this, "Give, and it will be given to you: good measure, pressed down, shaken together, and running over will be put into your bosom. For with the same measure that you use, it will be measured back to you" (Luke 6:38). God's emphasis is always on our receiving, not so much on our giving. Solomon's statement in Proverbs 3:10 about our barns being filled is an incredible statement. It all boils down to one question, "Who are we going to believe?"

We have the wisest advice ever given on stewardship by the wisest man who ever lived. He put it like this, "Honor the Lord with your possessions, and with the firstfruits of all your increase; so your barns will be filled with plenty, and your vats will overflow with new wine" (Prov. 3:9-10). What is the purpose of our stewardship? Are we honoring God? What is the product of our stewardship? Are we simply trying to be a steward of our time and talent and not with our treasure? God said the product of our stewardship is "our possessions." What is the priority of our stewardship? Remember, the first-fruits belong to Him. What is the promise of our stewardship? We can take Him at His word. However, the real question is not if we ask ourselves these four questions, but if we will act upon them. If we have not been regular tithers, will we begin to do so now?

The greatest stewardship verse in all the Bible is found in John 3:16, *"For God so loved the world that He gave His only begotten Son, that whoever believes in Him should not perish but have everlasting life."* The Lord Jesus was the product of the Father's stewardship to you. He was His only Son, the first-fruits of all those who would be born again after Him. We have a tremendous opportunity to honor God with our lives — the greatest of all our possessions. He said, "Those who honor Me, I will honor" (I Sam. 2:30).

Chapter Two

A God-honoring offering

What constitutes a God-honoring offering? If indeed the desire of our heart is to honor the Lord Jesus Christ with our time, our talents, and our treasures then the Biblical basis for a God-honoring offering is found in the 12th Chapter of John's gospel. The text unfolds a few days before Golgotha in a private home in Bethany. The little village of Bethany, on the eastern slope of the Mount of Olives, can still be visited to this very day. The Lord Jesus was reclining at the table with His disciples, His friend Lazarus, and others. Mary enters the room and brings to Him a God-honoring offering. She kneels at His feet, breaks open her alabaster box, and pours it out upon His feet. Then she wipes His feet with her hair. The fragrance of the perfume fills the room as tension fills the air. Judas is quick to rebuke her. But the Lord Jesus honored her. He blessed her gift and Matthew, Mark, and John all recorded it for posterity so that we might know what truly constitutes a God-honoring offering.

Four ingredients in a God-honoring offering leap from the pages of Scripture into our hearts as we read the text. A God-honoring offering is precious to us. Mary gave something very costly. It was not a token gift. It was precious to her. A God-honoring offering is pleasant to others. The whole house was filled with the fragrance of the perfume. Everyone got in on the joy of her gift. A God-honoring offering is perplexing to some. There will always be those like Judas who can't let go and give themselves. They are perplexed by those who can and do. Finally, a God-honoring offering is pleasing to Christ. He looked into her lovely face and exclaimed that she had done a beautiful thing to Him.

A God-honoring offering is precious to us.

 "Then Mary took a pound of very costly oil…"
John 12:1-3

An offering that honors the Lord must first of all be something that is dear to us. God is not honored by token gifts, by putting our finger in our own alabaster box and simply dipping and dabbing a little upon Him. A God-honoring offering is something that is precious to us. King David said this when receiving the offering to purchase the threshing floor for what would become the altar of the temple. He said, "I will not offer burnt offerings to the Lord my God with that which costs me nothing" (II Samuel 24:24).

When Mary brought her offering it was precious to her. Verse three refers to it as "very costly oil." It is also recorded that it was an offering worth three hundred denarii. One denarii was a day's wage in the first century world. Think of that! This lady brought the equivalent of one year's salary and poured it out upon Christ. It was beyond what was expected of her. It was beyond what many might have thought was reasonable. It was a God-honoring offering that was precious to her.

It is interesting to note that Mary's position was at Jesus' feet (John 12:3). This lady has center stage only three times in Scripture and each time she is at our Lord's feet. She sat at His feet to hear His word (Luke 10:38-42). She knelt at His feet in sorrow over the death of her brother Lazarus (John 11:32). She worshiped at His feet when she brought her offering (John 12:3).

What a wonderful place to be found . . . at Jesus' feet. Perhaps we should ask ourselves if we have been there lately? Have we been too busy? Too proud? Too self-reliant? It was Mary's favorite place. We see her there in times of sorrow. We see her there in times of joy. We see her there in times of receiving. We see her there in times of giving. We see her there when the sun is shining. We see her there when the storm clouds are gathering.

This lady's motive was love. The Bible records that her brother Lazarus was at the dinner party. We will quickly remember where he was in the previous chapter of Scripture. He was in the tomb! How grateful she was for what the Lord Jesus had done for her family. She came in love and she came with a grateful heart. She gave not out of duty but out of devotion. Love motivated her. This is a good point for us to ask ourselves if we have given anything to our Lord lately, not because we thought it was our duty, but out of deep devotion and gratitude. Whenever love exists in the heart there is a desire to sacrifice something for the object of our devotion.

A God-honoring offering is something that is precious to us.

This was no sudden impulse on Mary's part. She had "kept" this offering (John 12:7). The word is best translated "protected." She preserved it. She saved it. She kept it. She protected it. It was something that was precious to her. Mary came that day to pour out on our Lord what she had long treasured. She came to pour out upon Him something that was of value to her. God-honoring offerings always consist of something that is precious to us.

A God-honoring offering is pleasant to others.

 "...And the house was filled with the fragrance of the oil." John 12:3

"The house was filled with the fragrance of the oil" (John 12:3). The whole house was filled with this fragrance and not just the room in which they were seated. It had an effect on everyone who was present. Sooner or later everyone would know what had happened. Even those on the rooftop would know that something sweet had been offered below. Everyone in that house got in on the blessing that evening.

When we examine all the God-honoring offerings in the Bible we see that they are not just precious to us but they are pleasant to others. Mary's offering brought a blessing to others who were caught up in its fragrance. There is a very real sense that it was not simply a blessing to those in Bethany that evening but also to those of us today wherever we are. The Lord Jesus said, "Wherever this gospel is preached in the whole world, what this woman has done will also be told as a memorial to her" (Matt. 26:13). The offering she gave so long ago continues to be a challenge and blessing to us today. I think of the churches I have pastored and the godly men and women through the generations who have given so sacrificially whose offerings are still being blessed in so many ways today by others. I know young people who are provided scholarships because of the God-honoring offerings of those in years gone by. I know retired preachers and many of their widows who are living with dignity in their declining years because of the God-honoring offerings of those who have gone before us.

We encourage one another with our giving. When we hear of someone who makes a God-honoring offering it encourages us to do more. It becomes a challenge and blessing to us. The apostle Paul called the gift the Philippians sent to him "a sweet-smelling aroma, an acceptable sacrifice, well pleasing to God" (Phil. 4:18). A God-honoring offering is not simply precious to us but it becomes pleasant to others.

A God-honoring offering is perplexing to some.

 "...why was this fragrant oil not sold..."
John 12:4-6

Ironically, not everyone is blessed when others give God-honoring offerings. They are perplexing to some. A God-honoring offering exposes the phoniness in some people who begin to murmur like Judas and call it "a waste." Judas called Mary's offering just that — "a waste" (Matt. 26:8).

Perhaps there are still some today who would say the same thing to Mary that Judas said. That is, they would say it should have been sold and given to the poor. That type of criticism sounds so spiritual, doesn't it? Listen to Judas. Talk about audacity! Look at this phony. Talk about waste; he wasted his opportunity. He wasted his life. He wasted his very soul. He asks, "Why was this fragrant oil not sold for three hundred denarii and given to the poor?" (John 12:5). Doesn't that sound holy? Why was this not so? The answer is because what Mary had was not for sale, it was for sharing!

Some today in many churches say the same thing that Judas said. Had some been in Bethany that night they would have chimed right in. Oh, perhaps they don't say it with their lips but they say it with their checkbooks. Judas subtly used the excuse of the poor to bring more money into his own hands. This was the real issue. In fact, the Bible even says so — "This he said, not that he cared for the poor, but because he was a thief, and had the money box; and he used to take what was put in it" (John 12:6). There are still people like this today. Some people have a problem giving sacrificial and God-honoring offerings because they don't want to let go of their own money. So, like Judas, they use excuses not to give as a way of putting more money into their own pockets. Do you see the real tragedy here? Mary had just drawn all of the attention of the house to the Lord Jesus Christ. He was the center of attention. Judas turned the attention away from the Lord Jesus and put it on the poor. People like him give themselves away.

It is a fact of life that while God-honoring offerings are precious to us and pleasant to others they are certainly perplexing to some. They are perplexing to those who love money more than the Lord Jesus Himself. Churches are filled today with men and women who are as lost as Judas. He was not in love with the Lord Jesus Christ. He was in love with what was in his bag . . . money! John records that Judas took money out of Christ's treasury (John 12:6). He says he was "a thief." Here was a man putting his hand in Christ's own money bag and stealing from Him! But before we are quick to rise up in indignation, we must ask ourselves if we do the same thing. Malachi asks, "Will a man rob God?" When we ask, "How?" the answer comes back "in tithes and offerings."

Think about waste. The great waste comes in hoarding up things. The great waste comes in keeping them from their proper use. What if Mary's perfume had been hoarded up? Then it would have been wasted had it not been used. Here is a world in desperate need of the gospel and so many Christians are hoarding up estates, and never pouring any of it out on the Lord Jesus. Oh, once in a while we dip our little spoonful out as a token gift. Many will go to the grave with great estates but what good will it do them and what good will it do the gospel? Now, that is waste! Wasted resources. Wasted opportunities to be a blessing. Wasted resources that will be left to the government to fund illegitimate social programs and in some cases to heirs for whom it may become their own destruction. No, Mary's gift was not waste.

Men and women who are ruled by money will do anything to get it. For thirty pieces of silver Judas would later betray the Lord Jesus. Gehazi pursued Naaman for a talent of silver. The sorcerer Simon offered Simon Peter money for Holy Spirit power. The power money has over people can keep them out of heaven. No wonder Mary's offering was perplexing to Judas. He loved the money bag. It is interesting that Judas made such an issue out of Mary's gift and turned around the very next week and bargained with the chief priest to sell Christ for thirty measly pieces of silver.

A God-honoring offering is precious to those who give but perplexing to those who gripe. Where do you find yourself? Are you opening your hand to give to God what is precious to you or clutching tight to your possessions, perplexed by those who give God-honoring offerings?

A God-honoring offering is pleasing to Christ.

 "...For she has done a good work for me."
John 12:7-8; Matthew 26:10

While God-honoring offerings may be perplexing to some they are always pleasing to Christ. There was not a voice heard in the home that night in Mary's favor except one. It was the voice that really counted — the voice of Christ Himself. He looked into her lovely face and spoke to the others saying, "Why do you trouble the woman? For she has done a good work for me" (Matt. 26:10). When we give something that is precious to us it is always pleasing to Christ.

He said to those around, "Let her alone" (John 12:7). Matthew adds, "She has done a good work for me." Our Lord saw the broken alabaster box that was precious to Mary. It was worth a year's salary to her. He felt the oil on his feet. He smelled the sweet fragrance that filled the whole house and he said, "You have done a beautiful thing to me." Some people might call us crazy to do what Mary did. That is to give what we worked so hard to acquire. But our Lord Jesus calls it a "good work," a beautiful thing. It is pleasing to Christ. What about your alabaster box? Where is it? Is it locked safely away in a safety deposit box? It is invested in a stock portfolio? Is it tucked away in certificates of deposit? Or, is it poured out on the Lord Jesus Christ?

Our Lord Jesus emphasized the fact that Mary's gift was "for Me" (Matt. 26:10). This should always be an underlying reminder to all of us who give our tithes and offerings to our local churches and other various ministries. We are in reality giving to Christ Himself. It just so happens we are giving to Him through a local expression of His body that we call our local New Testament church.

Christ wrote Mary's biography that day. She never said a word with her mouth, but her biography was written that day. Earlier, our Lord had said, "Where your treasure is, there will your heart be also." Our Lord Jesus watches over the treasury (Mark 12:41). He looked at Mary and came to her defense with a word of sweet affirmation.

In Mark's account of this experience he adds that Christ

also said, "She has done what she could" (Mark 14:8). The fragrance of that perfume has long since evaporated but the memory of that woman will survive as long as the gospel is preached because she "did what she could." Mary's offering was pleasing to Christ because she did what she could. She could not keep his enemies from arresting Him in Gethsemene's Garden. She could not hold back the man with the cat o' nine tails who whipped His back. She could not hold back the hand of the man with the hammer who drove the spikes in His wrists and feet. But, she could identify with His cause. She could assure Him of her love. And "she did what she could."

What does the Lord Jesus expect of me? To do what I can! Our measure of faithfulness is not what someone else has done. We are to "do what we can do." All Moses had was a rod, but he delivered a nation. He did what he could. All David had was a slingshot. But he did what he could and slew a giant.

You say, "I don't have much." Then do what you can. Most of us don't do that much. Do what you can regardless of criticism. God-honoring offerings are perplexing to others. Do what you can regardless of the cost. God-honoring offerings are precious to us. Do it now, for the time is right. Do it now, for the time is short. Opportunities that are here today may be gone tomorrow. The widow of the gospels was the poorest of the poor, but she did what she could. Joseph of Arimathea was the richest of the rich, but he did what he could. They both gave to the Lord Jesus something that was precious to themselves.

The Lord Jesus said that what that woman did that evening

in Bethany would be written about, preached about, talked about, and read about everywhere around the world as long as the gospel is preached. And the fact that you are reading these words is the fulfillment of that prophecy in Bethany so many centuries ago.

Our Lord Himself reveals the truth of what constitutes a God-honoring offering. It is something that is precious to us. It is something that becomes pleasant to others. It is perplexing to some but mainly, it is pleasing to Christ.

Long before we ever thought of giving to God, God gave to us! Yes, He broke His own alabaster box and poured it out on you. His offering was precious to Him. It cost Him something dear. He gave His only begotten Son that we might have eternal life. Love is always expressed in giving something that is precious to us. God's gift to us is pleasant to others. We are a testimony of that today. The gift of Christ is what makes life worth living and fills whatever room we are in with the sweet fragrance of His love. His gift was perplexing to some. Some still look at the gift of Christ as Judas looked upon the gift of Mary and called it "waste." Some think that those of us who are followers of Jesus Christ are wasting our very lives in doing so. Finally, God's gift was pleasing to Himself. Isaiah 53:10 says, "It pleased the Lord to bruise Him." Mary broke her alabaster box because she knew He would not need a marble monument. He wasn't going to be in the grave long enough to even have a marker made.

It would do us all well to find our own place at Jesus' feet and say with missionary Jim Elliott of old, "He is no fool who gives what he cannot keep to gain what he cannot lose!"

Chapter Three

Economics 101

Every election year brings a new debate on the economy. If ever there was a subject with wide-ranging, dogmatic differences of opinion, it is the economy. My undergraduate degree is in Business Administration and I never shall forget my first college-level Economics course. There I learned the basic formula of economics that is called the law of supply and demand. It is a simple law. When demand exceeds supply, prices rise. When supply exceeds demand, prices decline. My Economics professor explained it in the following manner. Pretend there is a store that sells apples. On a given day there is a tremendous demand for apples. Outside the door there is a line of forty or fifty people waiting to buy apples. The supply of apples is low. What does the storeowner do? He raises the price of apples because the demand is exceeding the supply. On another occasion, there comes a time when there are a hundred apples in the store and no one has an interest in apples. There is no demand whatsoever. No one is asking for apples. They are about to rot and will become of no use to anyone. So, what does the storeowner do? He puts them on a sale table and lowers the price of apples because the supply is exceeding the demand. The law of supply and demand simply stated is that when demand exceeds supply, prices go up, and when supply exceeds demand, prices go down.

Now, what does all this have to do with Christ's feeding of thousands of people on the Galilean hillside? That experience was all about the law of supply and demand. Without Christ, demand always exceeds supply and the cry is "not enough!" With Christ, supply always exceeds demand and the cry is always "more than enough!" Of the thirty-eight parables that our Lord told in the gospels, one-third of them deal with our relationship to our own material possessions. One out of every six verses in Matthew, Mark and Luke discuss the right use of material goods. Our Lord reminds us that our money talks and is saying something about our commitment to Him.

One day our Lord laid out His economic plan for His people. He did not lay it out in the halls of government but on a green, grassy hillside in Galilee. That experience reminds us today that without Christ, demand always exceeds supply and the cry is "not enough." With Christ, supply always exceeds demand and the cry is "more than enough."

Without Christ demand exceeds supply and the cry is "not enough."

 "...Two-hundred denarii worth of bread is not sufficient..." John 6:1-9

A need had developed in Galilee. The demand was great. Thousands of people were gathered together far away from home without any food. There was no apparent supply to meet the demand. That is always the way it is without Christ. It may be that some reading these words are sitting on that hill this very day. Without Christ there is never enough. Demand always exceeds supply. Those who try to fill the void of life with money never have enough. How much is enough? Just a little more. How much sex is enough? Just a little more. How much recognition is enough? Just a little more. Why? Because the void of life is so large that only Christ can fill it.

There were three things that brought about this problem of demand and supply in Galilee. First, there was no sense of planning (John 6:1-5). These people did not think ahead. There were thousands of men, women, and children who had no sense of proper planning. They had a demand for which there was no apparent supply. The problem turned out to be an opportunity for the Lord Jesus Christ to work a miracle. In fact, all miracles begin at the platform of problems. The heartcry of so many today is "not enough." The reason is not that much different. There is no proper sense of planning for so many today.

They also found themselves in their predicament because they had no sense of purpose (John 6:5-9). Phillip and Andrew best illustrate this very fact. The Lord said that He was "testing" them (John 6:6). He had asked Phillip where they should buy bread to eat and John 6:6 reveals an interesting insight into our Lord. It says, "This He said to test him, for He Himself knew what He would do." Not only did he already know what he was going to do with Phillip and the multitudes, but he also knows what he is going to do with you and me. Our Lord was testing His disciples. Phillip gave an interesting response to Christ's question. He replied that "two hundred denarii worth of bread is not sufficient for them, that every one of them may have a little" (John 6:7). Phillip had a cash register for a mind. The first thing he thought about was not the glory of God nor the power of the Lord Jesus Christ, but how much would it cost? Not long before he had seen our Lord turn water into wine. However, Phillip dealt with the dilemma at hand the same way an atheist would. He looked only at what he could see. Give Phillip an "F". He flunked. He had no sense of purpose.

Andrew comes on the scene. He says, "There is a lad here who has five barley loaves and two small fish" (John 6:9). He is doing great thus far, but unfortunately he continues — "but what are they among so many?" Andrew crashes and burns. Give him an "F" also. Now Phillip and Andrew were both soul winners (Phillip found Nathaniel and brought him to Jesus, and Andrew found Peter and brought him to Jesus). But on the Galilean hillside they became part of the problem and not the solution because of no sense of purpose. Our Lord was testing them. I believe He was hoping they would say, "Lord, that is no problem for you. We watched you turn water into wine. You can do anything!" But neither Phillip nor Andrew figured Christ into the equation. Without Christ demand always exceeds supply. Phillip and Andrew are still around today. There are some who are ever looking over the scene for human possibilities to solve problems with their own resources. The disciples also found themselves in their predicament because they had no sense of potential (John 6:9). A lad comes on the scene who has a sack lunch with five barley loaves and two small fish. Look at that boy. He left home with enough to feed thousands of people and did not even know it. Demand often exceeds supply and it's not just because of no sense of planning or no sense of purpose. Sometimes it is because we have no sense of potential. Some reading these words left home this morning with unlimited potential and did not even know it. It is not the size of our lunch that matters but whether Christ possesses it. Little is much when God is in it.

Without Christ, demand always exceeds supply and our cry is "not enough!" Some of us have a need today for which there is no apparent supply. Perhaps it is material. Perhaps it is spiritual. Perhaps it is emotional. For Phillip, there was not enough money. Not enough bread. "Not enough," is the cry of so many today. Without Christ, demand always exceeds supply. Why? Because some of us, like those in Galilee, have no sense of planning. Others of us have no sense of purpose. And some of us have no sense of our own potential. Christ is "testing" us as He did those in Galilee. God has His own way of opening up heaven to those who figure Christ into the equation of life. It is the eternal law of supply and demand.

With Christ supply exceeds demand and the cry is "more than enough."

 "...Jesus took the loaves...and distributed them...and likewise the fish, as much as they wanted." John 6:10-15

We all know the story well. Jesus took the bread and fish, gave thanks to the Father, and multiplied it across the multitude. After everyone had eaten there were twelve basketsful of fragments that remained which were gathered. Yes, more than enough!

How did it happen? The boy gave (John 6:9-10). He could have clutched his brown paper bag, but he gave it to the Lord Jesus Christ. Jesus looked at the prospects. They were not much. Just a lad and a lunch. The boy planted a seed that day. He gave.

The boy gave all (John 6:11). He could have given one loaf and one fish and kept the rest for himself. But he gave everything that he had. That exchange between the lad and the Lord tapped the eternal resources of heaven and moved them into the bankrupt affairs of men. The lad reminds us today that he gave and he gave his all. And, then he stayed around to expect a miracle.

One of the most beautiful parts of this whole story is that the boy gave again (John 6:12-13). After everything was eaten there was more left over than there was to begin with. The boy would have the opportunity to give again. We never give anything to the Lord Jesus Christ and lose it. He gives it back to us again and again. Note the secret of God's own economy.

The boy gave to Jesus. The Lord Jesus gave to the disciples. The disciples gave to the crowd and the more they gave the more there was to give. And the crowd even had the opportunity to give back. The Bible says "they were filled" (John 6:12). Most of us would stop there. The need was met. Praise the Lord! But if it's great to get a blessing, it's greater to be a blessing. Jesus then says, "Gather up the fragments that remain." Now the people gave! The same ones who cried "not enough" are now crying "more than enough." Yes, with Christ supply always exceeds demand and the cry is "more than enough." There were twelve baskets of food left over. And the boy? He who gave so little would have the privilege of giving again. This is God's plan of economy.

It is interesting that Jesus said, "Gather up the fragments that remain, so that nothing is lost" (John 6:12). Note He said "so that nothing is lost." What did our Lord mean? This is the same Greek word that is translated "perish" in John 3:16. It is the same Greek word that is translated "ruined" in Matthew 9:17. It is the same word that is translated "perish or spoiled" in John 6:27. Our Lord Jesus wants us all to know that He is in the business of "picking up the pieces" of lost, spoiled, perishing, wasted, ruined lives, and using them again! He wants to gather up the pieces of broken lives today so that none will be wasted or lost.

Remember it's not the size of the lunch that matters but whether we are willing to let our Lord Jesus Christ have it all. The lunch did not do any good at all until it was placed in the hands of the Lord, and when it was, what a difference it made! Some of us who have been crying "not enough" have potential like a little lad and don't even know it.

Without Christ, demand exceeds supply and the cry is "not enough." With Christ, supply exceeds demand and the cry is "more than enough." Without the Lord Jesus Christ factored in the equation of life, we will never be satisfied. There will never be enough. When we ask ourselves how much is enough, we will always reply, "Just a little more." But with Christ, supply will always exceed demand and "more than enough" will be our theme.

Look finally at that little lad once more. He left home with enough in his little sack lunch to feed thousands of people and didn't even know it! Some of us say, "I can't do much. I am like a lad with a lunch." Then do what you can. The Lord Jesus Christ is not looking for your ability, but for your availability. We are full of potential. All we need for a miracle is a lad, a lunch, and the Lord. Little is much when God is in it!

Chapter Four

Robbery without a weapon

Malachi 3:7-12

As far-fetched as it may seem, our finances generally mark the position of our spiritual pilgrimage. We are no farther along in our walk with God than the point where we have learned to trust Him with our tithe. Someone has well said that more could be learned about a person's commitment by looking at their checkbook than their prayer book. This one area could be the reason for many unresolved conflicts and unmet needs.

The tithe is the place where many Christians go astray. Some because they have never been taught the spiritual truths concerning stewardship. Others because they have not studied the Word of God to find these truths for themselves. But mostly, because of willful rebellion against the Word of God. Many Christians profess to love the Bible and take it as their rule of faith, yet deliberately ignore the plain teaching of the Word of God regarding the tithe.

Now, please do not misunderstand. This chapter is not designed to get more money for the church or for God's work.

It is designed to lead the reader into spiritual growth and blessing by being obedient to the Word of God. One of the common complaints about many preachers is that they are always preaching about money. It is usually a telltale sign that those who are making these statements are generally the ones who are disobedient to God's Word regarding the tithe.

There is a lot of misunderstanding today concerning the tithe (one-tenth of our income belonging to God). In fact, one of the great injustices that many of us preachers have done to the church is to insist that God demands one-tenth of our income and one-seventh of our week. This implies that the other nine-tenths of our income and the other six days of the week are ours to do with as we please. The truth of the matter is that everything we have belongs to God. Not just the tenth — everything! We are nothing more than stewards passing through this world. For most of us, fifty years from now everything we own will be in someone else's name. Fifty years ago what you own today belonged to someone else...your land, your home, your assets. When you came into this world you came into it naked without a dime. And the obvious truth that follows is that you will leave this world the same way. We do not own a thing. We are merely stewards of God's resources. Consequently, the tithe is a great place to start in our stewardship with God. . . but it is a terrible stopping place.

As our text unfolds, we will see that the whole emphasis of the Word of God is not on our giving as much as it is on His opening the windows of heaven to pour us out a blessing there would not be room enough to receive. God wants to bless us far more than we want a blessing. The tithe is a starting place in getting God into action in the affairs of man. Let's venture into the realm of this exciting journey with God that promises to "open for you the windows of heaven and pour out for you such blessing that there will not be room enough to receive it" (Mal. 3:10).

God's apparent problem with us

 "…You have gone away from my ordinances and have not kept them…you have robbed me!"
Malachi 3:7-9

First, we note in our text *God's apparent problem with us!* "Yet from the days of your fathers you have gone away from My ordinances and have not kept them. Return to Me, and I will return to you," says the Lord of hosts. "But you said, 'In what way shall we return?' "Will a man rob God? Yet you have robbed Me! But you say, 'In what way have we robbed You?' In tithes and offerings. You are cursed with a curse, for you have robbed Me, even this whole nation" (Mal. 3:7-9).

We have before us God's problem with us. We see initially that this problem is *personal*. "YOU have robbed ME!" (Note the personal pronouns.) Have you ever been the victim of robbery? I talked recently with a lady whose home had been broken into, all her drawers ransacked, money stolen along with valuable papers, including her deceased husband's wedding ring and many sentimental items of great value. Her anguish was intensified by the fact that someone, uninvited, had invaded the privacy of her own domain and took items of value that belonged to her. You see, robbery is a very personal matter and only one who has been a victim of such an experience can know the real anguish of heart. God's apparent problem with us is personal. He said, "You have robbed Me." This is a strong accusation and not a mere insinuation. He calls to us in Malachi 3:7 saying, "Return to Me, and I will return to you." The point of return is always the point of departure. God said the place of departure for many of us is the matter of the tithe.

Here is God's apparent problem with us. It is robbery without a weapon. "YOU have robbed Me!" But the truth is when we rob God there are some other things we rob in the process. When we do not faithfully bring the tithe to God we rob the church of its ministry. We also rob the world of the gospel through great missionary enterprises. But even more personally, we rob ourselves of great blessings. "It is more blessed to give than to receive" (Acts 20:35).

In the New Testament we find these words escaping the lips of our Lord, "Render therefore to Caesar the things that are Caesar's, and to God the things that are God's" (Matt. 22:21). Is it not amazing that some church members would never entertain the thought of not paying their taxes (that is, rendering unto Caesar the things that are Caesar's)? Many of us would never think of not paying taxes on our home, sales taxes, or federal income taxes. And yet many of us never render unto God the things that are God's! This is *God's apparent problem with us*. It is a personal problem. We have robbed Him.

As we further examine the text, we see the problem is not only personal, but it is also *pointed*. God says, "You have robbed Me" (Mal. 3:8). We answer back, "How have we robbed You?" His answer comes in a very pointed way, "In tithes and offerings" (Mal. 3:8). Tithing is God's appointed program for us. It always has been, and it always will be. There are some today that say the tithe is merely an Old Testament law and is not applicable for this dispensation of grace. The truth of the matter is the tithe existed among the people of God long before the law was given. In Genesis 14:20, we see Abram giving tithes to Melchizedek. In Genesis 28:19-22, we see Jacob vowing to give a tenth unto the Lord. When the law was given the tithe was definitely incorporated in it. "And all the tithe of the land, whether of the seed of the land or of the fruit of the tree, is the Lord's. It is holy to the Lord" (Lev. 27:30).

In the New Testament we see Jesus approving and obviously practicing the tithe. The Pharisees were out to catch Him at any point they could. Certainly had Jesus been failing on the matter of the tithe, he would have had stern fingers of accusation pointed His way. Note what He says in His rebuke of the Pharisees in Matthew 23:23, "Woe to you, scribes and Pharisees, hypocrites! For you pay tithe of mint and anise and cumin, and have neglected the weightier matters of the law: justice and mercy and faith. These you ought to have done, without leaving the others undone." This verse is often misunderstood and misinterpreted. Here Jesus is rebuking the Pharisees for their hypocrisy, not for their tithing. In fact, He says, "These things you ought to do." The word "ought" is an imperative and is translated in other versions as "must." Jesus saw the tithe as a requirement from God. It is unthinkable in light of the cross on which our Savior died that any of us under grace would give less than the Jews gave under law!

I am amazed at many churches' mentality concerning the tithe. Some hand out pledge cards during stewardship campaigns asking the people to sign their names on a card promising to give an amount that "moves toward the tithe" or to pledge a certain amount that is not a tithe. This is astounding that we would ask people to promise to rob God!

It is helpful in our understanding of the tithe to know that it is holy unto the Lord. "And all the tithe of the land, whether of the seed of the land or of the fruit of the tree, is the Lord's. It is holy to the Lord" (Lev. 27:30). The Bible says that "the tithe is *holy* to the Lord." That is to say, God reserves for Himself, as His own, one-tenth of what He gives to us. It is holy to Him. There are not many things called *holy* in the Word of God. When something is set aside as holy it is a dangerous thing to keep that from the Lord. You may say you can't afford to tithe. The very reason you think you can't is no doubt because you have robbed God of something that is *holy* to Him.

Note that the text says, "The tithe is the Lord's!" (Lev. 27:30). This should open our eyes to a misconception that has blinded many from the truth of the Scripture that one-tenth of our income is not our own personal property at all. It does not belong to us. We have no say about it whatsoever. Regardless of what we have done with it, the tithe is the Lord's. God's tithe may be on your back in the form of a new suit of clothes. It may be in your home in the form of a new video game for your television set. You may be watching the Lord's tithe each evening on a big screen television set in your den. You may be driving the Lord's tithe down the street in the form of a new car. You may be investing the Lord's tithe in a bank or another investment institution. You may be stealing it, robbing it, driving it, wearing it, investing it…but it is still not yours…the tithe is the Lord's! It belongs to God, and in reality we do not give anything to Him until we give over the tithe.

We need to change our mentality toward the tithe. God says to withhold the tithe is the same as robbing His own treasury. It is indeed a penetrating question, "Will a man rob God?" Friend, I would rather rob the First National Bank than to rob God. It doesn't matter who we are or what we have, we need to tithe. The worse our financial condition, the more we need to tithe. The tithe is holy. It is the Lord's. According to the Bible, there is a blessing when we give it and a curse when we steal it. The Bible warns us plainly not to touch the tithe. We tithe because we love the Lord Jesus Christ. A Christian should tithe for the same reason he keeps all the other commandments. If we render unto Caesar the things that are Caesar's, let us also render unto God the things that are God's. God's apparent problem with us is personal and pointed.

God's appointed program for us

 "Bring all the tithes into the storehouse."
Malachi 3:10

Secondly, let us note *God's appointed program for us.*
"Bring all the tithes into the storehouse, that there may be food
in My house, and try Me now in this," says the Lord of hosts.
"If I will not open for you the windows of heaven and pour
out for you such blessing that there will not be room enough
to receive it" (Mal. 3:10).

If we are indeed guilty of robbing God of the tithe, then
certainly there must be some program of rehabilitation to
bring us into right relationship with Him. God lays down this
appointed program for us in the text above. Note first *the plan.*
"BRING all the tithes into the storehouse." Every word of
Scripture is important. Note that God told us to *bring* the tithes,
not *send* them. The Wise Men did not send their gifts of gold,
frankincense, and myrrh to the Christ Child; they brought
them. The woman with the alabaster box did not send the box
for Jesus' *anointing*; she brought it! God says that we are to
bring the tithe. There is personal worship in the act of bringing.
This is God's plan — "bring."

Second, note *the person.* "Bring YOU all the tithes into
the storehouse." YOU bring! You bring the tithe because you
are commanded to bring it, and love obeys. In the Scripture,
love is equated with action. Jesus asked, "Do you love
me?...feed my sheep." At another time He asked, "Do you
love me?...keep my commandments." He said, "He who

hears My words and does them, he it is who loves Me." Love is something we do. Love doesn't sing, "Oh how I love Jesus" — love tithes! You can tithe without loving, but you cannot love without tithing.

I am always a little intrigued by bumper sticker evangelism. We have all seen the bumper sticker that declares, "Honk if you love Jesus." However, the latest one that says, "Tithe if you love Jesus — anybody can honk!" contains a lot more truth.

Third, note *the proportion* in God's appointed program for us. "Bring ye all the TITHES into the storehouse." I Corinthians 16:1-2 says, "Now concerning the collection for the saints, as I have given orders to the churches of Galatia, so you must do also: On the first day of the week let each one of you lay something aside, storing up as he may prosper, that there be no collections when I come." Note the words, "as God has prospered him." This signifies a definite proportion of income. It does not say, "Let everyone lay in store as he feels led." Nor does it say, "Let everyone lay by in store as he feels moved by the Holy Spirit." Friend, the Holy Spirit will never lead us to do anything contrary to the Word of God. And the Word of God teaches us that the tenth is the Lord's. The Bible says, "Let everyone lay by him in store as God has prospered him." That is, in a proportionate way, according to a percentage basis. This makes giving equal. The millionaire and less wealthy person are equal in their giving in relationship "as God has prospered." Thus, we see that the proportion of our giving is the tithe.

Next, the text reveals to us *the place* of our tithes. "Bring ye all the tithes into the STOREHOUSE." Where is the storehouse? Again, I Corinthians 16:1-2 says we are to "lay in *store*." This clearly points us back to Malachi 3:10 which says for us to "Bring all the tithes into the..." what? Into the storehouse! Also note that we are to do this "upon the first day of the week." What happens on the first day of the week? Obviously, the local New Testament church is at worship. And the truth of the Scripture is that the local church is the storehouse! In the New Testament, over ninety percent of the time the word *church* is mentioned, it refers to that local, first-day worshipping body of baptized believers. It is not our privilege to scatter our tithe around to all sorts of parachurch or evangelism organizations, youth groups, etc. They are to receive offerings, not tithes! The tithe is to be brought to the local New Testament church, the storehouse, on the first day of the week. And by the way, don't sell the church short. It will still be here when all the other organizations and groups are dead and gone. Any organization that does not originate in, cooperate with, and build up the local New Testament church will come to nought. The place of the tithe is the storehouse — the church.

The text also reveals to us *the purpose*. "Bring all the tithes into the storehouse THAT THERE MIGHT BE MEAT IN MY FATHER'S HOUSE." The purpose of bringing the tithe is to further the work of Christ through the church in bringing salvation to men and women. This is our good and godly purpose given to us by the Lord Jesus Christ in the great commission.

Finally, note *the proposition*. "Bring ye all the tithes into the storehouse that there might be meat in my Father's house, and PROVE ME." This is unbelievable! God is saying to you, "Put me (Almighty God) on trial. Prove me, try me, with the tithe!" This is one directive in the Scripture that can be put on a trial basis. We are challenged to return to Him the one-tenth that is rightfully His and see whether or not He will let us be the loser. This is amazing condescension that God allows Himself to be put on trial by us in such a manner. If there is any doubt as to God's existence, here is the way to prove Him. What a proposition — prove me, put me to the test!

God's appointed program for us is definitely the tithe. The tithe is a great place to *start*, but a miserable place to *stop* in our stewardship. In fact, in the purest biblical sense, a tither is simply a reformed thief.

God's abundant provision for us

 "…pour out for you such blessing that there will not be room enough to receive it." Malachi 3:10-12

What happens when we become aware of God's apparent problem with us, and meet the conditions of God's appointed program for us? Note finally *God's abundant provision for us!*

"Bring all the tithes into the storehouse, that there may be food in My house, and try Me now in this," says the Lord of hosts, "If I will not open for you the windows of heaven and pour out for you *such* blessing that *there will* not *be room* enough to *receive* it. And I will rebuke the devourer for your sakes, so that he will not destroy the fruit of your ground, nor shall the vine fail to bear fruit for you in the field," says the Lord of hosts; "And all nations will call you blessed, for you will be a delightful land," say the Lord of hosts" (Mal. 3:10-12).

Oh, the promises of God that are ours for the claiming! We see first that there is *the promise of provision*. God says to us that He "will open the windows of heaven and pour us out a blessing that there will not be room enough to receive." There has never been a time when we more needed to know how to open the windows of heaven than today. Remember that these promises are contingent upon our returning to God in the matter of the tithe.

Note that this promise of provision involves *quality*. These blessings come right out of heaven. They are supernatural. God says, "I will open the windows of heaven, and pour you out a blessing." He will "pour out." They will be sudden. Have you ever poured tea from a pitcher? If you are not careful it will pour out in rapid force. God says our promise of provision will be right out of heaven. What does it mean that He will "open the windows of heaven?" Let Scripture interpret Scripture. Listen to Genesis 7:11-12: "In the six hundredth year of Noah's life, in the second month, the seventeenth day of the month, on that day all the fountains of the great deep were broken up, and the windows of heaven were opened. And the rain was on the earth forty days and forty nights." Here the identical expression is used. This same expression used with the deluge of the flood is the same expression used in Malachi 3 in God's response to our tithe. God has promised to honor us with an abundant outpouring! We are not talking about only spiritual blessings, but temporal blessings. The truth of the Scriptures is that we "reap what we sow." If we sow oats, we will reap oats. If we sow wheat, we will reap wheat. The laws of the harvest simply stated are that we always reap what we sow, we always reap after we sow, and we always reap more than we sow. Surely we do not suppose the Lover of our Soul will allow us to be the loser because we are faithful to His Word and obedient to His will. I have never seen nor heard of a consistent tither who did not find this to be true. The reason so many are in financial straits today is the simple fact that they have robbed God.

The promise of provision not only involves *quality*; it involves *quantity*. Notice the quantity of the blessing "there shall not be room enough to receive it." This simply means we shall have to give it away. This "more than enough blessing" is for all that meet His conditions. Isn't this a far cry from the haunting need today where so many are crying "not enough?" Man's rebellion leads to this kind of economy…the cry of not enough! But not God's. His abundant promise to us is that He will open the windows of heaven and pour out a blessing for us that we will not have room enough to receive. This is the John 6 principle in action. The boy gave his lunch of a few fish sandwiches and thousands of people were fed and basketsful were left over. John Bunyan is reported to have said, "There was a man; some called him mad; the more he gave; the more he had!" This is God's promise of provision in a nutshell, involving quality along with quantity.

There is also the *promise of protection* involved here. God says, "I will rebuke the devourer for your sakes." This is quite a promise! When we return the tithe to God we step into the supernatural protection of God. I confess to you that I do not know all the ramifications of this promise. However, that does not mean that I do not choose to abide in the promise that God will supernaturally give protection. If the devourer is a plague on our crops, God says He will devour him, "I will rebuke him." If the devourer is recession, God says, "I will rebuke him in your behalf." God gives supernatural protection to the consistent tither. It is His abundant promise to us.

We are not commanded to tithe because God is dependent upon our gifts of money. This brings the wrong concept of our sovereign God. He is certainly not dependent upon you or me. The truth is, God doesn't need our money. He commands us to tithe in order that we might get involved in His program of economy that unlocks the floodgates of blessing upon us. The whole significance of this passage of Scripture is that when the tithe is presented it releases the vast treasures of heaven and moves God into action in our behalf. It always has and it always will!

God's apparent problem with us is obvious. It is personal. "You have robbed me." It is pointed. "In tithes." But God doesn't leave us in this sad condition, for we see His appointed program for us. The plan "bring," the person "ye," the proportion "all the tithe," the place "into the storehouse," the purpose "that there will be meat in my Father's house," and the proposition "and prove me." Almighty God is saying to us, "put me on trial. Prove me herewith…tithe!" And once we have met this program we see God's abundant promise to us — the promise of provision and the promise of protection. "If you return to me…I'll return to you." This is God's promise to you today.

The tithe is the Lord's. It is holy unto Him. And He led the way. The greatest stewardship verse in the Word of God is found in John 3:16, "For God so loved the world that He gave His only begotten Son, that whoever believes in Him should not perish but have everlasting life." In light of the cross upon which our Savior died, the question of our text has penetrating proportions. "Will a man rob God?"

Many say, "I know I need to be obedient to God with the tithe, but I just can't seem to get started." The following are a few simple and proven practical suggestions as to how to begin:

(1) Make it a matter of definite prayer.

(2) Give the tithe priority over everything else. The Bible speaks of our giving of "the firstfruits." Each time you deposit your paycheck make sure the first check you write is "unto the Lord."

(3) Be just as strict and systematic with the tithe as you are in business matters. In fact, even more so, for it belongs to God.

(4) Always rest in the fact that we can trust the Lord. There has never been a consistent tither who was sorry he tithed.

The Lord Jesus gave Himself for you and will not allow you to be the loser because you are faithful to His Word and obedient to His will.

(5) Go ahead...do it! "Prove me," says the Lord, "If I will not open the windows of heaven and pour you out a blessing that there will not be room enough to receive it." (Mal. 3:10) "Return to me, and I will return to you" (Mal. 3:7).

Chapter Five

Your money talks… what does it say?

James 5:1-6

"Come now, you rich . . ." With these four words James begins his discussion of Biblical stewardship (James 5:1-6). Many of us are prone to skip over this paragraph, erroneously feeling that it does not apply to us. We think this passage is for the men and women who live in the multi-million dollar homes on the water. We may think, "Yes, Lord, give it to those rich snobs!"

There are basically two reactions to James' discussion of money. Those without money somehow feel that they are more spiritual than those who have money. Well, they are not. On the other hand, those who have money somehow feel as if they have to be defensive. Well, they don't. These verses apply to everyone, for being "rich" is relative. Compared to the rest of the world, almost everyone reading this book is filthy rich. Most of us have automobiles with power steering. We can afford to buy hamburgers for lunch. Most of the world's people cannot.

I wish I could take each of you out into the African bush a few miles from Mombasa, Kenya, in East Africa. I have preached in some churches there. It is not uncommon for three or four thousand people to walk miles to attend the services. They sit on the ground, not on pews. If their pastor were to preach on James 5:1-6 this coming Sunday, they would be thinking about people in America who make the minimum wage when they heard the words, "Now listen you rich people..."

No matter how much we have, someone else has more. No matter how little we have, someone else has less. These words in James 5:1-6 are for each of us. I know many poor people who are more preoccupied with money and possessions than some wealthy people are. The real issue is not whether we have money, but whether money has us. James was touching a sensitive nerve regarding the danger of materialism — being possessed by things.

Many of us think that money is all we need to solve our problems. We think if we just had a little more money we could take care of this, or take care of that, and then we would finally be happy. But what happens when money comes? The more money we have, the more we need. The more we make, the more we spend. We get a raise and usually it just helps us get a little more in debt. Money is deceptive. It can so subtly and unconsciously become our god. If we are not careful, it begins to possess us instead of our possessing it.

There is nothing wrong with wealth itself. Genesis 13:2

says, "Abram was very rich in livestock, in silver, and in gold." In I Chronicles 29:28 it says that the psalmist David "died in a good old age, full of days and riches and honor." King Solomon, the writer of Proverbs, had more than Abraham and David put together. Joseph of Arimathea, who furnished a tomb and arranged for our Lord to have a decent burial, had tremendous wealth (Matt. 27:57). Barnabas, a wealthy landowner, made possible the expansion of the early church by selling some valuable real estate on the island of Cyprus and giving the proceeds to the apostles. No wonder his name means "son of encouragement."

If there is nothing wrong with wealth, what was James saying? He was trying to tell us that the problem with wealth lies not in having it, but in how we get it, how we guard it, and how we give it. The way we deal with our money can bring "misery" upon us (James 5:1). The word "misery," when translated, comes from two Greek words. One means "to undergo or to endure," the other means "callous, or that which brings joy only momentarily, but is followed by misery." Getting our money by ungodly means will bring misery sooner or later. If we hoard our money we will be of all men most miserable. And if we give our money to self-indulgence, the result will be misery. James did not say that wealth in itself is wrong. We should not misunderstand what he was saying. His point was how we get our money, how we guard it, and how we give it tells the whole world what our values are.

Our money talks. In fact, it says volumes about what we

really think is important. It is so much a reflection of what is inside us that Jesus spoke often about it. One out of every three of His sermons had to do with money. Jesus told thirty-eight parables, and one-third of them dealt with possessions. He said, "Where your treasure is, there your heart will be also" (Matt. 6:21). He was a diagnostician. And in a very real sense, the accountant who prepares our tax return knows more about us spiritually than our Sunday School teachers or prayer partners know. How we deal with our money is a reflection of our spiritual health.

How we get it

 "Indeed the wages of the laborers who mowed your fields, which you kept back by fraud, cry out; and the cries of the reapers have reached the ears of the Lord of Sabaoth." James 5:1, 4, 6

The issue of how we get our wealth is so vitally important that the thought pervades the first paragraph of James 5. When writing this passage, James had in mind a man who received his money through exploitation and expropriation.

James said, "Indeed the wages of the laborers who mowed your fields, which you kept back by fraud, cry out; and the cries of the reapers have reached the ears of the Lord of Sabaoth" (James 5:4). The Bible never condemns the acquisition of wealth by legal and legitimate means. At issue here is the acquisition of wealth by illegal and illegitimate means. The man who received his wealth through exploitation had promised to pay his employees a certain amount, but when they completed their work he refused to pay them. The phrase "failed to pay" is a translation of a Greek word that refers to an illegitimate or fraudulent action. From the very beginning, this man had no intention of paying his workers. He was always looking for loopholes in the contract to get out of paying what he owed. Because of this he came under God's judgment.

Throughout the Old and New Testaments, God warns us, "Do not defraud your neighbor or rob him. Do not hold back the wages of a hired man overnight." Deuteronomy 24:14-15 tells us, "You shall not oppress a hired servant who is poor and needy, whether one of your brethren or one of the aliens who is in your land within your gates. Each day you shall give him his wages, and not let the sun go down on it, for he is poor and has set his heart on it; lest he cry out against you to the Lord, and it be sin to you." Exodus 2:23 tells us that God heard the cries of the slaves in Egypt: "Then the children of Israel groaned because of the bondage, and they cried out; and their cry came up to God because of the bondage." In Luke 10:7 Jesus says, "The laborer is worthy of his wages."

The tense of the verbs in James 5:4 is important to the understanding of the verse. The verb translated "mowed" is aorist, indicating the task had been accomplished. The verb translated "failed to pay" is in the imperfect tense, indicating that the employer held back the wages permanently and had no intention of paying what was due. The verb translated "crying out against you" is in the present tense, indicating the continuous crying out of these wages. The employees began to cry out to God about this injustice. We will see later that payday comes sooner or later.

Remember the term "rich" is relative. We do not have to be employers to be guilty of exploitation. Some employees exploit their employers. For example, suppose your employer pays you for eight hours of work a day. You show up ten or fifteen minutes late, take an extra five minutes on your morning and afternoon breaks, come back from lunch fifteen minutes late, sit at your desk and read a magazine or do your nails, and then leave a few minutes early. You have only put in about six and a half hours of work, not the eight you agreed to work. You are just as guilty of exploitation as the man who did not pay a fair wage. If your employer pays you for an eight-hour day and you only work seven hours, you are stealing from him. You might as well go into the petty cash box and take out the money.

Christians in the work force ought to work harder than anyone because they are doing their jobs unto the Lord (Eph. 6:5-8). Ill-gotten gains will come back to haunt us. We must guard against acquiring our wealth through exploitation.

James made a stinging accusation: "You have condemned, you have murdered the just; he does not resist you" (James 5:6). The man James had in mind not only gained his wealth through exploitation but also through expropriation. The Greek word translated "condemned" is a judicial term suggesting the manner in which the rich pervert the legal system to accumulate their wealth. The term speaks of those who control the courts in such a way that justice is eliminated. In other words, they have the power to use the courts to take away someone else's means of support. The man who exploited his workers had the political power to control the system and prevent his employees from opposing him. Thus he deprived them of their livelihood. It was just as if he had murdered them.

There are ways of killing people without taking away their physical lives. We can kill a person's reputation through slander. We can kill a person's incentive through constant agitation. James was thinking of a man who stepped over anything or anyone in order to reach the top.

The victims did not offer opposition because the system controlled by the rich rendered them unable to retaliate. James 2:6 says, "But you have dishonored the poor man. Do not the rich oppress you and drag you into the courts?" To exploit is bad enough, but it is worse still to expropriate when resistance is impossible. In the end, wealth gained by expropriation can only bring misery.

We cannot help but remember that the love of money was at the root of Christ's betrayal. Judas loved money. Yes, he received thirty pieces of silver and look how he got it. He is the epitome of someone who ended up weeping and wailing.

Yes, our money talks. What is it saying about how we got it? If we have obtained our wealth through exploitation or expropriation, our gold and silver will testify against us.

How we guard it

 *"...You have heaped up treasure in the last days."
James 5:1-3*

How we guard our money is also revealing. The man James had in mind "hoarded" his wealth (James 5:3). "Hoarded" is a translation of a Greek word from which we get our word "thesaurus." It means "a collection" and has the connotation of gathering all we can and storing it up. There is nothing wrong with a savings account. In fact, the Bible puts its stamp of approval on fiscal responsibility. See II Corinthians 12:14 for an example. However, it is wrong to hoard wealth that is owed to others. James said that guarding such wealth is deceitful, decadent, and deceptive.

Guarded wealth promises joy, but only brings misery. When we begin to love money it ceases to bless us and begins to curse us. We think that just a little more money will make us happy, but that is a deception.

The parable of the rich fool illustrates the deceitfulness of guarded wealth. Jesus said, "So is he who lays up treasure for himself, and is not rich toward God" (Luke 12:21). The man in the parable accumulated wealth "for himself" with utter disregard for anything or anyone else. So God said, "Fool! This night your soul will be required of you; then whose will those things be which you have provided?" (Luke 12:20). We sometimes think a new suit, a new car, or a new home will make us happy. But these things never really satisfy. They are all deceitful. It is good to have things money can buy, but it is better to have the things money cannot buy. Behind mahogany doors and iron gates are some of the most miserable people in the world. What is really important is not what money can buy, but what money cannot buy.

Andrew Carnegie, who will always be remembered as one of America's greatest entrepreneurs, said, "I was born in poverty and would not exchange its sacred memories with the richest millionaire's son who ever breathed. What does he know about a mother or a father? These are mere names to him. Give me the life of the boy whose mother is nurse, seamstress, washer woman, cook, teacher, angel, and saint all in one, and whose father is guide, exemplar, and friend. No servants to come between. These are the boys who are born to the best fortune. Some men think that poverty is a dreadful burden and that wealth leads to happiness. What do they know about it? They know only one side. They imagine the other. I have lived both, and I know there is very little in wealth that can add to human happiness beyond the small comforts of life. Millionaires who laugh are rare."

Yes, hoarded wealth is deceitful.

Money can also be decadent. It decays. If we don't use it, we lose it. We cannot take it with us when we die. It is temporal. Only what we deposit in the bank of Heaven will last. That which is used for God's glory never fades away. Jesus says, "Do not lay up for yourselves treasures on earth, where moth and rust destroy and where thieves break in and steal; but lay up for yourselves treasures in heaven, where neither moth nor rust destroys and where thieves do not break in and steal" (Matt. 6:19-20).

Emphasizing the perishable nature of worldly riches, James 5:2-3 says, "Your riches are corrupted, and your garments are moth-eaten. Your gold and silver are corroded, and their corrosion will be a witness against you and will eat your flesh like fire. You have heaped up treasure in the last days." All three verbs are in the perfect tense. James was so certain of the temporary nature of riches that he described their decay as having already happened. He was showing us the present worthless state of our possessions.

The first century world did not have certificates of deposit or stock certificates. Their wealth was measured in grain, garments, and gold. When James said, "Your wealth has rotted," he was referring to grain. A man's worth was often determined by the amount of grain he could store in his barn. Remember the rich fool had many goods laid up for future years. But grain rots. How does grain rot? By lack of use. Our guarded wealth, like grain, is decadent. If we don't use it, it does us no good and we eventually lose it.

When James said, "Moths have eaten your clothes," we know that in the ancient world garments were also symbols of wealth. When Joseph blessed his brothers in Egypt, he gave them garments (Gen. 45:22). Lust for a Babylonian robe led to the downfall of Achan (Joshua 7:21). Naaman, commander-in-chief of the Syrian army, brought Elisha garments as a gift (II Kings 5:5). The man James had in mind made his money for the express purpose of showing off to others how rich he was; he wanted to be noticed by his fancy and flashy outer garments. (The Greek word "himatia," translated "clothes" in James 5:2, means "outer garment.") But garments ruin. Moths eat them.

A moth is subtle and silent, lurking behind the scenes. He eats away at our treasures and before we know it they are gone. A moth is not like other insects. A roach will badger and taunt us. He will eat away at our cabinets and leave his droppings on the drain board. A cricket will bug us (no pun intended) by making noise and remaining hidden. A mosquito will bite us. A fly will bother us. But a moth will beguile us. He keeps to himself. He will not badger, bug, bite, or bother us. He will not gnaw at us or make a lot of noise. He will simply hang out in the back of the closet and work in secret until it is too late.

Moths eat our clothes when they hang in our closets for long periods of time. Garments ruin because of lack of use. Likewise, when we guard our wealth instead of using it, it decays. We do not see our riches being eaten away, but before we know it they are gone.

Grain rots, garments ruin, and gold rusts. James 5:3 says, "Your gold and silver are corroded." Again, it is lack of use that causes decay. A hinge on a gate that hasn't been opened in a long time can become corroded. A pair of pliers left outside can gather so much rust that they can hardly be opened. The Greek verb translated "corroded" is singular, indicating that James was speaking of gold and silver as a symbolic unit.

He was talking about assets that symbolize our wealth. The Greek preposition *kata* (the first part of *katiotai*) means "through," indicating that the gold and silver are completely corroded. The point of the illustration is that unused wealth that is hoarded and guarded is decadent.

Most of us know that real gold will not rust. Therefore, James was also saying that our wealth is actually fool's gold. It has no eternal value. What a disappointment to discover that what we thought was valuable is worthless. Guarded wealth is both deceitful and decadent.

Wealth brings a false sense of security. The stock market is up one day and down the next. Money markets and financial accounts fluctuate from hour to hour. Riches are uncertain. James' contemporaries experienced firsthand the deceptiveness of guarded wealth. Within a decade after James wrote his epistle, Jerusalem was destroyed by the Romans, and the Jews' accumulated wealth was taken. This siege in A. D. 70 brought famine and disease. The situation was so bad that those who had been wealthy before were now reduced to demoralizing and depraved activities such as cannibalism.

It is a mistake to think that security is found in wealth. It is also a mistake to think that it is good stewardship to guard our wealth. James 5:3 says that our corroded gold and silver will testify against us. Wealth is deceptive. The man James had in mind guarded his wealth in self-defense, but in the final analysis his wealth was used against him. How ironic. The question at the judgment seat of Christ is not going to be,

"How much did you make?" The question will be, "What did you do with what you had?" Your money talks!

Hoarding our wealth affects not just ourselves, but others as well. James 5:3 says, "You have heaped up treasure in the last days." The last days began with Christ's ascension and will end with His second coming. We may be nearing the end of the last days. The question is, "How will we use our wealth in these days of tremendous evangelistic opportunity?" Too many of us guard wealth rather than give it to the Lord's work.

James reminded us that these guarded resources will testify against us and eat our flesh like fire. They will expose us. This is a serious warning, not an irrelevant addendum. James' words ought to make us sit up on the edge of our seats. There are many people who do not believe that ultimately they will be punished by God. They think of God only as a God of love. However, the same God who says that He is a God of love says that He is a God of justice.

God is as concerned with how we guard our wealth as He is with how we get it. What are we going to do with the money that we have hoarded up? One day each of us is going to die and someone else is going to spend it. In many cases, our money will only cause our heirs misery because it will take away their incentive to work. Our influence for good or bad will continue after we are gone. All the accounts are not in yet. This is why our judgment awaits Christ's return. We will not be judged as soon as we die.

It is a great tragedy to come to the end of life and have

treasure laid up in this world only. We came into this world without anything and we will leave the same way. We do not own our possessions. They all belong to God; we are but stewards. People who hoard the possessions they think they own will one day weep and wail in misery (James 5:1).

Their problem was not in possessing money, but in letting it possess them. Money is not the root of all evil. Paul said, "The love of money is a root of all kinds of evil" (I Tim. 6:10). Those who are deceived into loving money will covet. Although "You shall not covet" (Ex. 20:17) is the last of all the Ten Commandments, it may be the most dangerous command to break. Covetousness makes a person break the other nine commandments. David broke the seventh commandment — "You shall not commit adultery" — because he broke the tenth and coveted Bathsheba. Gehazi broke the eighth commandment — "You shall not steal" — because he broke the tenth and coveted Naaman's riches.

There is nothing wrong with money, but money that is guarded will never spread the gospel of Jesus Christ. However, money in the hands of a good steward can be a testimony. At the end of your life will you be considered a hoarder or a steward? Your Last Will and Testament is your last testimony. It is read at the end of your life, and it says what is really important to you. What does your will say as a testimony of Jesus Christ?

How we give it

 "You have lived on the earth in pleasure and luxury;..." James 5:5

Our money talks primarily by how we give it. Some people simply give their money to themselves in self-indulgence, while others give it to the Lord to advance His kingdom. The man James had in mind gave his ill-gotten gains to himself. He "lived on the earth in pleasure and luxury" (James 5:5). The word for "luxury," means "extravagant comfort, to lead a soft life." The word for "self-indulgence," means "to give oneself to pleasure." It is also found in I Timothy 5:6: "But she (the widow) who lives in pleasure is dead while she lives." (See Jesus' parable of the rich man and Lazarus in Luke 16:19-31 for another example of someone who lived in luxury.)

James 5:5 continues, "You have fattened your hearts as in a day of slaughter." This image communicates well to me because I grew up in Fort Worth, Texas, where the famous stockyards are on the north side of town at the beginning of the Old Chisholm Trail. If you were to walk the streets of the north side today you would see steers penned up in the stock-yards. They are given the finest of grain and do not realize that they are going to be slaughtered. Consequently, they eat and eat and eat, taking the pleasures of the moment. And the more they eat the quicker they will be led to the slaughterhouse. When they are all fattened up, the workers throw a little corn in front of the stupid steers and their desire for self-indulgence and luxury entices them right out of the pen and into the slaughterhouse next door.

James was saying that some of us are like those Texas steers. We just keep fattening ourselves, not knowing that we are hastening the day of our own slaughter. The slaughterhouse represents the judgment to come. Those who guard their wealth and give it only to themselves are blind to the fact that they are headed toward a day of reckoning. They follow their selfish appetites and are too blind to see that it is to the ruin of relationships or to the ruin of self-respect.

There are some supernatural laws that should govern our giving. There is the *law of clarification*, which states that God owns all the wealth in this world and the next. In David's words, "For all that is in heaven and in earth is Yours" (I Chr. 29:11). "The earth is the Lord's, and all its fullness" (Ps. 24:1).

The *law of circulation* states that God wants His wealth in circulation. In God's economy the earth had one theme in the beginning: give, give, give. The sun gave. The earth gave. The animals gave. The man gave. The trees gave. But Satan came and introduced a new concept: get, get, get. Man became greedy and began to live by Satan's philosophy, but God's original design for the use of resources still applies.

The *law of cooperation* states that all of God's wealth belongs to His children. The problem is that they are not cooperating with Him. Paul said, "We are heirs — heirs of God and joint heirs with Christ" (Romans 8:17).

Finally, the *law of cultivation* states that the way to appropriate God's wealth is to give. We never reap until we sow.

Jesus says, "Give, and it will be given to you: good measure, pressed down, shaken together, and running over will be put into your bosom. For with the same measure that you use, it will be measured back to you" (Luke 6:38). To coin a phrase, we are to "give out of God's hand." We are to reach into His unlimited resources and give from Him to others. What a privilege. Perhaps King David said it best: "For all things come from You, and of Your own we have given You" (I Chr. 29:14).

We live in a world where accumulation is the name of the game. Caught in this trap, many of us get everything we can and guard it as long as we can. Some of us foolishly think that the issue at the judgment bar of Christ will be, "How much have you accumulated?" or "How much have you guarded?" However, let's not for a moment think that our Righteous Judge will look at us and ask, "How much did you make?" His question will be, "What kind of steward were you? What did you do with what I gave you?"

The fundamental danger inherent in having wealth lies in the fact that it can cause us to focus our complete attention on this world. We may begin to live for this world alone. Once we possess wealth, it may begin to possess us. The Christian must beware of this danger. He must get his wealth honestly, guard it loosely, and give it selflessly to Christ.

As we have seen, it is not what we guard but what we give that makes us rich. When we guard earthly treasure it rots, ruins, and rusts. And one day it will stand up to testify against us. Yes, your money talks. Does it say, "Get me any way you can, whether it be through exploitation or expropriation?" Does it say, "Guard me, hold me tight, keep me, clutch me?" If so, you of all people are most miserable. Does your money say, "Spend me on yourself and no one else?" If so, it has become your master. Or does it say, "Give me away to others in the service of Jesus?" If so, you know the peace and joy that can only come from Jesus Christ.

Chapter Six

Lord, do it again

Ezra 8:21

"Then I proclaimed a fast there at the river of Ahava, that we might humble ourselves before our God, to seek from Him the right way for us and our little ones and all our possessions" (Ezra 8:21).

It is interesting how throughout history bodies of water, and in particular, rivers, seem to mark spots not only of reflection but also spots of embarkation to new opportunities and challenges. For Julius Caesar it was the Rubicon River. He stood there in 49 B.C. The order came to disband his armies and give up the struggle to conquer Rome. He pondered the dilemma. He could give up and give in or cross the river and press on. However, once the Rubicon was crossed, there could be no turning back. Caesar made his decision and the rest is history. For George Washington it was the Delaware River. On Christmas night, 1776, he crossed the Delaware and marched on the enemy troops at Trenton. He went on from there to establish the greatest and most unique nation in world history. For General George Patton it was the

Rhine River. This river marked a significant crossover point in the fall of Nazi Germany.

The fact that bodies of water often mark spots of embarkation to new opportunities and challenges is never truer than within the pages of the Bible. Moses had his Red Sea. For him it was the point of embarkation out of bondage toward the Promised Land. Joshua had his Jordan River. It was the crossover point into the Land of Promise and new challenges and opportunities. Elijah had his own Brook Cherith which prepared him for a life of ministry and power. For Jacob it was the river Jabbok. Israel sat down by the rivers of Babylon, hung their harps on the willows, and lost the song in their heart as they were captive to Babylon.

As the remnant of the children of Israel left their captivity, they made their way back to Jerusalem under the leadership of Ezra. They never made a more important stop on their pilgrimage en route to restoring and repairing their lost heritage than the stop at a little known river mentioned in only one chapter of the Bible called the river of Ahava. They once knew such glory. Jerusalem! The Temple! But for a time they had been taken into captivity, stripped of their pride. They hung their harps on the willow trees and could not sing the Lord's song in a foreign land. But now they were returning under the leadership of the likes of Ezra and later Nehemiah. Yes, they were returning to be used of God in restoring the glory of the house of the Lord.

We often hear a lot about what happened when the

remnant returned to Jerusalem. In Nehemiah's book we read how the walls were completed and how Ezra stood to read the Word of God, and all the people gathered as "one man" in the square and wept as they heard the Word of God. However, we seldom hear about one of the most important parts of their journey. They made a strategic stop along the way. Ezra "gathered them by the river that flows to Ahava, and camped there three days" (Ezra 8:15). The Bible goes on to record that Ezra "proclaimed a fast there at the river of Ahava, that we might humble ourselves before our God, to seek from Him the right way for us and our little ones and all our possessions" (Ezra 8:21). They stopped at the river of Ahava to seek the Lord for two things — to humble themselves and to find the right way home.

These men and women had been through difficult times. Their leadership had failed them in the past. They had some leaders that were more interested in self-serving than they were in leading the people. Their leaders had used their people to build their own positions instead of using their positions to build their people. They had been without direction for a period of years. They had hung their harps on the willow trees. They had no spirit of conquest. They longed "for the good old days." Now Ezra comes on the scene and God appoints him to lead them back to Jerusalem to restore their lost heritage. He is no real hero. He is simply God's appointed leader in God's own time.

There is a sense in which we see many of our own

churches' pilgrimages here. Like Israel of old, we know what it is to have seen the glory. Perhaps some of us have had leadership difficulties in the past. Some have hung their harps and longed for the good old days. Sometimes we forget how greatly God has blessed our churches.

We are on the march. But we need to make an important stop at our own river of Ahava. Why? To humble ourselves and seek from Him the right way for us; He is not through with us yet. We also are going to seek the right way for "our little ones," those who are coming after us, and seek the right way from Him for "all our possessions." It is interesting that Ezra adds this in Ezra 8:21 along with seeking the right way for our families. Why does He deal with our possessions? Because Jesus said, "For where your treasure is, there your heart will be also" (Matt. 6:21).

We are living in a time when churches all over the Western world need a new paradigm, one that goes beyond the traditional dimension of properties and buildings and programs, a new paradigm that touches a world. As many of our churches stand at the banks of the river of Ahava, we have a unique opportunity. What has happened to many churches in America over the last twenty years? One of the reasons God has blessed us in so many ways is that we have given ourselves to so many people and so many ministries outside our walls. Our world mission projects literally are around the world today. They are out there from hospitals in India to seminaries in Canada, hundreds of other projects where our churches have given so sacrificially not only of our money but also of our time and talents. We have not awakened to the fact that our own local bases are in need. Like Jerusalem, some of our own walls are beginning to break down. This is particularly true in some of our children's areas. Many have already lost a couple of generations to the church.

The Western church needs to camp here at our own river of Ahava for a while. Why? "Then I proclaimed a fast there at the river of Ahava, that we might humble ourselves before our God, to seek from Him the right way for us and our little ones and all our possessions" (Ezra 8:21). When I was pastor of First Baptist Church in Dallas, we called a fast. There was nothing legalistic about it. We challenged each other to fast on Fridays (sundown Thursday to sundown Friday). Then we received a love offering for some much-needed remodeling of our present facilities and upgrading of much of our equipment. As pastor, I certainly could identify with Ezra who went on to say, "So I was encouraged, as the hand of the Lord my God was upon me; and I gathered leading men of Israel to go up with me" (Ezra 7:28). As pastor in Dallas, I lived with these words of Ezra for the many weeks we challenged our people according to Ezra 8:21.

Many people in our churches have disposable income. Giving a worthy offering on a special day for some is not much of a sacrifice. Others wonder, "Where will we ever get anything extra to be able to give to the Lord through this offering?" I remind you of the words of Solomon in Proverbs 13:23. He said,

"Much food is in the fallow ground of the poor." What does this mean? Fallow ground is ground that hasn't been plowed or planted in a long time. The Bible says there are resources available of which we're not even aware but will be as we pray and fast and seek the Lord's will and way. One of our deacons related to me the story of a lake lot that he had owned for years. It had simply been sitting there with nothing happening, and it dawned on him that this lot was "food in the fallow ground" that he could sell and bring to the Lord's offering. There is probably enough jewelry in safe deposit boxes in Dallas that hasn't been taken out in years to educate all of our young preachers and send all of our missionaries to the field!

When Moses raised the money for the building of the tabernacle, the people prayed, met God in the offering, and brought their offerings for God to Moses in such a fashion that he had to stand up finally and say, "Please don't bring any more. We have more than enough for the task." Yes, Lord, do it again! Do it again, Lord, like you did in I Chr. 29 when David raised the money for the temple in Jerusalem. Do it again Lord like you did when Ezra went back to rebuild the walls of Jerusalem. Ezra said, "The freewill offering of the people and the priests, are to be freely offered for the house of their God in Jerusalem" (Ezra 7:16). LORD, DO IT AGAIN!

Lord, do it again. What will it take? It will take four things to awaken the church. The "where" is important. The "what" is impassioned. The "why" is imperative. And, the "who" is implicit.

The where is important

 "Then I proclaimed a fast there at the river of Ahava,…" Ezra 8:21

It was "there at the river of Ahava" that Ezra camped with his people for a certain period of time. They were on their way out of years of bondage. Ahava preceded the blessing of the rebuilding of the temple. As they camped at Ahava, they were not what they were going to be, but they were not what they used to be either. There is a sense in which most of us find ourselves at this strategic point of our journey at our own river of Ahava.

These men and women of old were about to make a momentous decision to leave the relative security and comfort of a life in exile to which they had become accustomed and comfortable. This can happen in a church when they've lived without really being challenged for a period of time. The Jews in exile under Artaxerxes found favor and were granted permission to take a remnant back to the Holy City. The river of Ahava was a separating point between the two places. It was the place along their journey where they either went forward or turned back to be content with an existence outside Canaan.

The church stands on the banks of our own river of Ahava. We can exist a few more years as we are, but we will not settle for that. We have seen the glory in the past. We're at a place in our own pilgrimage that calls on us to do the impossible and become true crossover people. As we stand at our river, we can look both ways. We can look to Babylon which would be the easy route. It's the way that calls for no real sacrifice. Or, we can go on up to Jerusalem where the Lord has called us. The "where" is an important point along our journey. Ahava is the deciding point.

There are many of us at our own personal river of Ahava, that place where we must decide to go on or turn back, for some of us in relationships with others or even in our relationship with Jesus Christ. The "where" is important. The river of Ahava is the separating point.

The what is impassioned

 "...I proclaimed a fast..."
Ezra 8:21

What did Ezra do there at the river of Ahava? He "proclaimed a fast." They fasted for three days. They were impassioned. If the Lord is to do it again with us, it will take our men and women beseeching Him with prayer and fasting. Fasting most often appears in the Bible in connection with prayer. Down through the centuries the people of God have practiced fasting; that is, doing without food for a certain period of time. Why? To focus our attention on our prayer need. To allow every simple hunger pain to remind us of our point of prayer. It is a personal discipline. People in Bible days fasted at many times and for many reasons. They fasted on the Day of Atonement. They fasted in times of need, such as war (Judg. 20:26; I Sam. 7:6). They fasted in times of sickness (II

Sam. 12:16). They fasted in times of mourning (I Chr. 10:12). They fasted in times of repentance (Neh. 9:1). They fasted in times of danger (Esth. 4:3,16). They fasted in times of preparation for ministry (Ex. 34:28; Dan. 9:3). In the midst of fasting the Bible warns about making it a show for others to see (Jer. 14:12). In fact, Jesus rebuked the religious phonies of His day who put ashes on their faces to look long and drawn during days of fasting so that people might look upon them and see them as spiritual. He told us when we fasted that we should wash our face and get well groomed so as not to be a show for those around (Matt. 6:16-18). True fasting is always accompanied by prayer, humility, and confession. God seems to honor our turning aside from time to time from ordinary pleasures and pursuits in order to humble ourselves before Him and to seek from Him the right way.

Ezra stood on the banks of the river of Ahava with the vision of rebuilding the broken walls. He had a vision of what could lie ahead for the Jewish people. Therefore, he called his people to get on their knees and to seek God in humility for the right way. A leader is not a leader without a vision and without calling his people to prayer. There's never been a greater need for us to get on our knees and stay there until God directs each of us His way as we plead with Him to "do it again." The "where" is important. It was there at the "river of Ahava," the separating point. The "what" is impassioned. They got serious in seeking the Lord with prayer and fasting.

The why is imperative

 "…that we might humble ourselves before our God, to seek from Him the right way…" Ezra 8:21

Why did Ezra proclaim a fast at the river of Ahava? That he and his people might humble themselves before God and seek from the Lord the right way. They could have gone back to Jerusalem with self-determination and pumped up positive mental attitudes with the idea that "we can do it" in our own strength. Or, he could have played the guilt game and sought to get the people to give of their time and treasures and talents through motivating them by guilt. He could have played the grudge game and sought to get them to give out of a grudge, not because they wanted to, but because they felt they had to. Instead, we join him in simply beseeching the Lord and learning more about grace giving — meeting God in the offering and giving as He puts it upon our hearts.

Why should we fast? To humble ourselves before God. And to seek from Him the right way, to depend upon Him. It is imperative to seek from Him the right way. The Hebrew translation means that we are to seek from Him the straight journey, the direct road so that we would not be turned aside by those who seek to get us off track. There are always those people in the Bible and people today who seek with their own agendas to try to get us onto detours, dead ends, cul-de-sacs, or even side streets. The "why" is imperative. For us, it is to humble ourselves before God as a church and to seek from Him the right way.

The who is implicit

 "...for us and our little ones and all our possessions." Ezra 8:21

Now, for whom are we going to beseech God over the next few weeks? First, for "us." Sometimes when we've been a Christian for years, we think we no longer need to seek from Him the right way for ourselves. Some Christians seem to get on automatic pilot and sail along through the Christian life with nothing ever being fresh and new in the way of seeking from God the right way day by day. There are a lot of things in our own personal lives and in our church life for which we need to seek the right way for us. There are many prayer needs at this particular point of our juncture. God is not through with us yet. There are some who have been coasting for a time, some who are just waiting to get back in the joy of the Lord. We need direction individually.

This is for us. Every single one of us is important to God. No one else has a fingerprint like mine, or a DNA like yours. There are many people in our churches who do not have much time left to do something big for God. Many of our people have resources that ought to be in God's work.

Ezra says we are to seek the right way not only for us, but also our "little ones." Ezra was wise enough to know that there was a whole generation coming after them for whom they had a responsibility. We used to sing a song that spoke volumes to my heart. The song related our hope in saying, "May all who come behind us find us faithful." Many of us rejoice in the wonderful church facilities we have had through the years because of the tremendous sacrifice of those who went before us. Now we must pass the baton to the next generation, and I wonder if those who come behind us will find us as faithful as those from whom we've enjoyed the blessings over these last years. Many of us have children and grandchildren who will learn about Christ and receive Him as a personal Savior in our churches. Our children and the children of adults we will reach in the future may never know the true way unless we cross our own river of Ahava and are faithful in our own stewardship. Some of us have never had to make significant sacrifices for what we've enjoyed for years. Someone else did — another generation. But now it is our turn. When Israel was on their way back to Jerusalem, they were called upon to "Go through, Go through the gates! Prepare the way for the people; build up, build up the highway! Take out the stones, lift up a banner for the peoples!" (Is. 62:10). They were to prepare the way, pave the way, and point the way. But why? They were already on the way. They were already there. They built up the highway and left the banners to point the way for those many who were coming after them. We too have an obligation to pave the way so it will be easier for those who come after us to get home. It is no wonder, Ezra said, that we were to seek the right way not only for us, but also for "our little ones."

Finally, he said we were to seek the right way from God, for us, our little ones, and "all our possessions." It dawned on them that they were stewards and that they needed God's direction, the right way, not only for themselves and their children but for all their possessions. We are but stewards passing through this world. We own nothing. We are but stewards. Some of us have sought the right way for ourselves and for our children, but have never thought of asking God what we should do with our possessions.

It is interesting that Ezra adds this phrase about our possessions. The Lord Jesus reminds us that "where our treasure is, there our heart will be also." So, as they were on the way back, they were to fast and pray about their possessions.

The children of Israel never had a more important stop on their pilgrimage back to rebuild the glory of Jerusalem than at the river of Ahava. Nor will we at our own river of Ahava. It is the place where we proclaim a fast, humble ourselves, and seek from Him the right way for us, our little ones, and for all our possessions. Ezra 8:23 records, "So we fasted and entreated our God for this, and He answered our prayer." I pray that this verse will be written all over our churches. In fact, this has been the testimony of God's people down through the centuries. Ezra goes on to say that, "Then we departed from the river of Ahava on the twelfth day of the first month, to go to Jerusalem. And the hand of our God was upon us, and He delivered us from the hand of the enemy and from ambush along the road" (Ezra 8:31). The Jews returned to Jerusalem, and they turned over their treasures. The journey which began with a fast ended with a feast, and the chapter concludes with these words, "So they gave support to the people and the house of God" (Ezra 8:36).

Here we are. Lord, do it again. What will it take? It will take stopping by our own river of Ahava on the way back. The "where" is important. It will take getting serious with God in prayer and fasting. The "what" is impassioned. It will take humbling ourselves before God and seeking from Him the right way. The "why" is imperative. Finally, it will take seeking the right way for us, our children, and all of our possessions. The "who" is implicit.

Chapter Seven

Modern money myths

II Corinthians 8:1-7

Many approach the subject of stewardship with long, drawn-out apologies. I have never apologized for my leadership responsibility at this point. In fact, we do people an injustice if we do not lead in teaching Biblical principles of stewardship. Greed is one of the biggest obstacles to personal and corporate revival. When the back of greed is broken, the human spirit soars into regions of spiritual awakening. Ask a little lad with a little lunch. Ask a lovely lady with an alabaster box. Ask our Lord Jesus Himself. In the 8th Chapter of the II Corinthian letter, the apostle Paul talks about our stewardship. His emphasis is not on our giving by guilt because we have to. Nor is his emphasis on giving with a grudge because we ought to. But his emphasis is upon giving with grace because we want to. He even begins with grace in the first verse of II Corinthians 8. The Corinthian church was not giving to the Lord's work. When we are not spiritual we are generally not generous. Paul encourages them by using the Macedonians as an example. The Macedonians had suffered greatly for the faith, and yet they gave so sacrificially for the Lord's work. They excelled in what Paul called "the grace of giving" (II Cor. 8:7).

As Paul wrote these words, the Jerusalem church was being scattered throughout the world. There was a depressed economy. However, the Greeks in Corinth were doing well financially. But, they were not giving to the Lord's work as they should. Thus, the apostle writes and uses the Philippians, the Bereans, and the Thessalonicans as examples to them. Little did those Macedonians know when they gave what they did that they would influence us two thousand years later.

Now, there are some modern money myths from Corinth that need to be dispelled today. The Corinthians were living with these myths and seeking to justify their lack of giving to the Lord's work because of them. In so many ways the church of the Western world today is living with these same money myths.

Myth number one — only people with money should give

 "...their deep poverty abounded in the riches of their liberality." *II Corinthians 8:2*

Some people say only people with money should give. Let Bob or Bill do it. He has the money. We often exclaim, "If I had their money I would give; I would tithe." Yes, myth #1 is that only people with money should give. But that is just a myth. Paul said that these people gave out of "a great trial and out of deep poverty." They gave out of what? Stock reserves? Certificates of deposit? Savings? No, out of "deep poverty"

and "great trial." The Greek word translated "trial" in II Corinthians 8:2 is the same word that means purging. The word picture is of a precious metal that is heated until the liquid impurities rise to the top and are scraped off. Pure metal is left and when it is cool it's stronger than ever. Here were people who were being tested. The heat was being turned up on them. Yet, out of this great trial they gave to the Lord's work.

The apostle also says that they gave out of "deep poverty." The word means "rock bottom destitution." They had lost their jobs. But circumstances did not keep them from giving. The people in Macedonia did not buy into the myth that those in Corinth did, that only people with money should give.

Our Lord Jesus destroyed myth #1 when he encountered the widow with her last coins. We all know the story well. A lot of people would counsel her to keep it. They would tell her that only people with money should give. And they would have robbed her of a great blessing and us of a great example. Our Lord placed that widow with a few pennies in the Bible to show us that our money talks. He still sits opposite the treasury to see not what we give but how we give it. She gave out of her want and not out of her resources. How many times have we heard, "Only people with money should give?" I have had people tell me that if I had a million dollars, or if I won the lottery, I would give to the Lord's work. If God can't trust you to give out of poverty how will He ever trust you to give out of riches?

It is a myth that says that only people with money should

give. The greatest givers are most often those with little. This is because it is not what we give, but how we give, that matters most to Christ. Look at the Macedonians. What an example they are to us today. They gave out of "great trial and deep poverty."

Myth number two — it is unpleasant to give

 "...that in a great trial of affliction the abundance of their joy and their deep poverty abounded in the riches of their liberality."
II Corinthians 8:2

Some say it's unpleasant to give. Many think we would be happier if we kept our money for ourselves. Some people believe we should "give until it hurts." That is a myth. There is great joy in giving. It is said of the Macedonians that they gave with "the abundance of their joy."

The Lord Jesus destroyed myth #2. He said, "It is more blessed to give than to receive." Think about that at Christmastime. When you and your family are all around the tree opening gifts, what do you do? Do you watch the one who is opening the gift? I don't. I watch the giver. I watch the expression on the giver's face who is filled with delight when they see the recipient enjoying the gift they have given. It is written all across their face! This is why parents like Christmas so much. Because it is fun to give! The only reason some of us have not found the "abundance of joy" in giving is because we simply have not practiced it.

It is a myth to say that it is unpleasant to give. Those who know what it is to have an open hand with God have joy. We remember back in Bethany this very expression of blessing. Jesus said to the woman in Bethany that she had done "a beautiful thing to Him." She walked home on a cloud with joy in her heart that night. Have you given anything lately that caused the Lord Jesus to say, "You have done a beautiful thing to me?" Look at the Macedonians. They gave out of an "abundance of joy." It is a myth to say that only people with money should give, and it is an equal myth to say that it is unpleasant to give.

Myth number three — giving results in a lack of resources

 "...their deep poverty abounded in the riches of their liberality." II Corinthians 8:2

Some fear that if we give we will not have enough for ourselves. It is a myth to say that giving results in a lack of resources. Some of us never add the supernatural into the economic equations of life. This is myth #3. Jesus Himself said, "Give, and it will be given to you: good measure, pressed down, shaken together, and running over will be put into your bosom. For with the same measure that you use, it will be measured back to you" (Luke 6:38). Listen to the message of the Macedonians — "In a great trial of affliction the abundance of their joy and their deep poverty abounded in the riches of their liberality" (II Cor. 8:2). Some of the richest people I know are poor, and some of the poorest people I know are rich! Some have what money can buy, and some have what money cannot buy.

The Lord Jesus destroyed myth #3 one day in Galilee when He took a little lad and a little lunch and taught us all a lesson. The boy left home with all of the potential of the world that day and didn't even know it. His giving started a chain reaction. He gave to Christ. Christ gave to the disciples. The disciples gave to the crowd. The crowd gave back to the disciples. And all because the boy gave "beyond his ability" (II Cor. 8:3). He "abounded in riches."

It is a myth to say that giving results in a lack of resources. Many who are reading this can attest to that very fact today. The fact is often our lack of giving is what results in our lack of resources. God will never allow us to be the loser when we are faithful to His word and obedient to His will. There are many modern money myths from Corinth that need to be expelled.

Myth number four — just do what you can

 "...and beyond their ability, they were freely willing." II Corinthians 8:3

No, you can do more than you ever imagined you were able to do. Listen to the message of the Macedonians. "For I bear witness that according to their ability, yes, and beyond their ability, they were freely willing" (II Cor. 8:3).

Some people give today in a strange way. They sit down. Add up all their bills. Pay them all. Set aside money for incidentals. Put aside money for their monthly recreation activities. Then at the end of the month if anything is left over, they give it to the Lord Jesus and His church. They are the ones who say, "Here is what I am able to do." Thus, this type of individual never tithes and never benefits from God's plan of economy. He buys into myth #4 from Corinth that you should just do what you can do.

Long years ago, my wife Susie and I learned the truth of this myth. We have learned through the years that we could not only do what we were able to do but along with the Macedonians "beyond our own ability."

It is a myth to say that you should just do what you can do. When you say that, you leave God out of the equation of life. I don't necessarily know exactly how it works, but those of us who practice it know it's true. It is a miraculous thing to be able to "give from God's hand." David said, "Everything comes from You and we only give You what comes from Your hand!" (I Chr. 29:14-16). A lot of people today are like the Corinthians who justify their lack of giving with modern money myths. But they are only that — myths. It is a myth to say only people with money should give. It is a myth to say it is unpleasant to give. It is a myth to say giving results in lack of resources. It is a myth to say, "Just do what you can do."

Myth number five — you have to give; giving must be coerced

 "...they were freely willing..."
II Corinthians 8:3-4

Some say you can't get people to give without putting pressure upon them. Some use gimmicks. Others use guilt. Some try to make us feel like we have to give, while others try to make us feel like we ought to give. But that is a myth. Stewardship is voluntary. Stewardship is a privilege. Listen to the message from Macedonia — "I bear witness that according to their ability, yes, and beyond their ability, they were freely willing, imploring us with much urgency that we would receive the gift and the fellowship of the ministering to the saints" (II Cor. 8:3-4). These Macedonians saw it as a privilege to give. They were "freely willing" to give. Wow! They begged for someone to take their offerings. They got more excited about the offering than they did any other part of their worship. The grace of giving will open our hearts, but it will also open our hands.

It is a myth to say that we have to give. Those committed to Christ see giving as a grace and a privilege.

Myth number six — we give to other causes to help them

 "...but they first gave themselves to the Lord,..."
II Corinthians 8:5

Some people give today by saying, "Here is a need; let's give to this need and help this cause or help this particular person." But that in itself is a myth! Look at the Macedonians. Look at their priorities. They saw it not so much as giving to others as a gift to God Himself. Paul says, "They first gave themselves to the Lord, and then to us by the will of God" (II Cor. 8:5). This is what makes Christian giving different from any other kind of giving. Some people give "A Day's Pay the United Way." Others give to the Salvation Army. As followers of Jesus Christ we give ourselves first to Him. Our giving is always to the Lord. The Lord Jesus said, "Inasmuch as you do it unto one of these the least of mine, you do it unto me." When David was raising the money to build the temple he said, "I have seen with joy how willingly your people who are here have given to you" (I Chr. 29:17).

Myth #6 says that we give to other causes to help them. No, in Christian stewardship we give ourselves first to the Lord, and then our resources. If our priority is giving ourselves over to the Lord then we will have no problem with giving our resources. This is why many churches have such a high level of stewardship participation. They have a high level of personal discipleship and devotion.

How should we then give? Some are miffed today by

modern money myths from Corinth. Where do we get our motivation in stewardship? Paul relates it in the context of these verses when he says, "For you know the grace of our Lord Jesus Christ, that though He was rich, yet for your sakes He became poor, that you through His poverty might become rich" (II Cor. 8:9). Our Lord laid aside His glory and became poor. He did not begin in Bethlehem. He became poor. He laid aside His glory and stooped down to earth. He veiled his deity in a cloak of humanity. Why? Because the Son of God became the Son of Man in order that "for your sakes He became poor that you through His poverty might become rich." What ultimately matters is not what money can buy but what money cannot buy. Christ is who makes us rich!

Paul said, "You know the grace of our Lord Jesus Christ." Do you? He did not leave heaven gritting His teeth nor clenching His fists. He did not leave shouting to the Father, "Okay, okay." No, it wasn't obligation that caused Him to give. It was grace! They did not drag Him up the Via Dolorosa screaming and kicking. No, they led Him like a sheep to the slaughter. Yes, we know the grace of our Lord Jesus Christ, that though He was rich, yet for our sakes He became poor that we through His poverty might become rich." And, that is our motivation for Christian stewardship. No wonder Paul concludes his discourse on giving in II Corinthians by saying, "Thanks be to God for His indescribable gift!" (II Cor. 9:15).

Chapter Eight

For such a time as this

I Chronicles 29:1-20

I had the unique privilege of being pastor of two churches which have had long and illustrative histories, the First Baptist Church of Fort Lauderdale, Florida, and the First Baptist Church of Dallas, Texas. Time and again our spiritual forefathers have risen to the occasion when the hour of need has come. Down through history those before us have sacrificed and served that we might enjoy the benefits of their labor. We are deeply indebted to them. Our children have had the opportunity to be saved and grow up in the faith of God through these ministries because so many sacrificed so much in years gone by. Now, the baton has passed to us. We must do the same for the twenty-first century! May our children and grandchildren look back upon us and remember us as a people of faith. We have come to the kingdom "for such a time as this."

One of the most informative, instructional, and inspirational passages in all of Scripture is found in the twenty-eighth and twenty-ninth chapters of the first book of Chronicles. David and his people were confronted with a challenge similar to the one facing those of us who are expanding church buildings. The time had come to build the temple in Jerusalem. It was to be the physical edifice where God would meet his people. After all the years in Egyptian bondage, after all the years of wilderness wanderings, after all the years of conquering Canaan, through the times of Judges and the reign of Saul and David, at last the glorious moment for the building of the temple had come. King David seized the opportunity to raise the money for the building of the magnificent edifice where Jehovah God would meet with His people for centuries to come.

David knew his whole life had been meant for that one special moment. What if you knew your whole life was meant for one special moment? What if you knew that all of your life God had prepared you to give and to prepare "for such a time as this." Like Esther who would come after him, David had come to his kingdom "for such a time as this." No wonder it was so easy to lead his people to give the necessary funds for the construction of the temple. It was the opportunity and moment of a lifetime, and God's hand was upon him.

How did the Israelites do it? How did they raise such a vast sum of money for the building of the temple? They followed seven vital principles to victory. How can we do it as a family of faith? The answer is found in the pattern and principles left for us by the ancient Israelites. They left us some scriptural guidelines for supernatural giving "for such a time as this." These guidelines have to do with the occasion of our giving, the order of our giving, the origin of our giving, the object of our giving, the opportunity of our giving, the objective of our giving, and the outcome of our giving.

Principle number one: The occasion of our giving

 "...the temple is not for man but for the Lord God."
I Chronicles 29:1

"Furthermore King David said to all the assembly: 'My son Solomon, whom alone God has chosen, is young and inexperienced; and the work is great, because the temple is not for man but for the Lord God'" (I Chr. 29:1).

Was the building of this magnificent temple something David thought up himself? Was it the brainchild of his constituency? No, a thousand times no! The occasion of their giving was God-caused. God had initiated the need of the temple and God had given David the plan for building it.

Consider the following Scriptures: "And the plans for all that he had by the spirit, of the courts of the house of the Lord, of all the chambers all around, of the treasuries of the house of God, and of the treasuries for the dedicated things" (I Chr. 28:12). "All this," said David, "the Lord made me understand in writing, by *His* hand upon me, all the works of these plans" (I Chr. 28:19). "And David said to his son Solomon, 'Be strong and of good courage, and do it; do not fear nor be dismayed, for the Lord God — my God — will be with you. He will not leave you nor forsake you, until you have finished all the work for the service of the house of the Lord'" (I Chr. 28:20).

God had caused the need and God had given David the

plan for carrying it out. The temple was not the imagination of a man's mind. It was initiated and orchestrated by God himself. The occasion of the Israelites giving was God-caused and God-directed.

David placed before his people the greatness of the task. He said, *"The work is great"* (I Chr. 29:1). People then and people now want to be a part of something that is great for God! Yes, the task is great for us. Do you know why some people in some churches never give of their resources willingly and joyfully? They do not believe the work is great. For some of them it has become a mere ecclesiastical ritual to be performed on Sunday morning so they might see themselves as respectable.

When we built a new church plant in Fort Lauderdale I asked our people some questions. Do you think what God is doing through our First Baptist Church is important? Do you think it is a great work? Do you think it is not for man but for God? If so, you realize the occasion of our giving like the Israelites is God-initiated and not man-initiated. David gives us the true reason why the work was great. Why? Because "the temple is not for man but for the Lord God" (I Chr. 29:1). This is why we were involved in that great work in Fort Lauderdale. It was not for us; it was for a testimony to God. Into the twenty-first century and long after every one of us is in heaven, people by the tens of thousands will pass those facilities and see that there was a people of faith who responded to a God-caused need who rose to the occasion of raising up a cross in the heart of a hell-bent, sinful city. The work is great! Why? Because "the temple is not for man but for the Lord God."

What is the occasion of our giving? God's blessings brought about our needs. We were a God-blessed people. We would not need new facilities if we were a dead church. We would not need new facilities if we did not sense the urgency of the hour in reaching masses of men and women for Christ. We would not need new facilities if we existed solely for those who are here now, instead of those who are yet without our walls. We would not need new facilities if we had no vision. The truth is, we did not create the need. God did! The need before us was an invitation from God for each of us to discover how wonderfully He can provide.

The building of new facilities did not originate with us. We did everything we could for ten years to keep reaching people for Christ without constructing buildings. When one Sunday School was full we started another, then a third. When one worship service was full we started a second, and then a third. God's blessings and the impression of His Spirit upon our hearts brought about our needs. And since God's former blessings brought about our need, we could be sure that God's future blessings would be sufficient to meet the needs the former blessings caused!

What is the occasion of our giving? Like the Israelites, God has taken the initiative. The occasion of our giving is God-directed and God-initiated. This is an important principle to victory.

Principle number two: The order of our giving

 "...I have given to the house of my God...my own special treasure...Then the leaders...the captains...with the officers over the kings' work, offered willingly." I Chronicles 29:2-9

"Now for the house of my God I have prepared with all my might: gold for things to be made of gold, silver for things of silver, bronze for things of bronze, iron for things of iron, wood for things of wood, onyx stones, stones to be set, glistening stones of various colors, all kinds of precious stones, and marble slabs in abundance. Moreover, because I have set my affection on the house of my God, I have given to the house of my God, over and above all that I have prepared for the holy house, my own special treasure of gold and silver: three thousand talents of gold, of the gold of Ophir, and seven thousand talents of refined silver, to overlay the walls of the houses; the gold for things of gold and the silver for things of silver, and for all kinds of work to be done by the hands of craftsmen. Who then is willing to consecrate himself this day to the Lord? Then...the leaders of the tribes of Israel, the captains of thousands and of hundreds, with the officers over the king's work, offered willingly. They gave for the work of the house of God five thousand talents and ten thousand darics of gold, ten thousand talents of silver, eighteen thousand talents of bronze, and one hundred thousand talents of iron. And whoever had precious stones gave them to the treasury of the house of the Lord, into the hand of Jehiel the Gershonite. Then the people rejoiced, for they had offered willingly, because with a loyal heart they had offered willingly to the Lord; and King David also rejoiced greatly" (I Chr. 29:2-9).

The proper order of our giving is a vital principle to victory. Note who led the way in giving. The people? No. The leadership? No. David himself, the leader. David said, "I have given my own special treasure of gold and silver" (I Chr. 29:3). David told his people what he and his family were going to do. He was giving out of his personal treasures. Some men are used to doing things out of expense accounts. David did not take money out of the government treasury to meet a need. He gave of his own personal treasures. It is interesting that David told them exactly what he and his family were going to do. He let them know he was giving one hundred twelve and a half tons of gold and two hundred sixty-two and a half tons of silver. What led David to give so liberally and sacrificially? He had "set his affection upon the house of his God." He had devoted his heart to it.

David did not simply give his personal time. There are a lot of leaders who do that. Nor did David simply give of his personal talent. Still other leaders do this. David gave of his personal treasure for the construction of the temple and it was over and above his regular giving. Note the order of the giving. First, David gave. Then the leadership gave. Then the people gave.

Examples are vitally important. Here we see David setting the example. He is practicing what Gideon preached when he said to his men, "Do as I do." It is the same principle Paul would use later when he wrote to the Philippians and said, "The things which you learned and received and heard and saw in me, these do, and the God of peace will be with you" (Phil. 4:9). It was the same principle Paul used when he wrote the Corinthian church saying, "Imitate me, just as I also imitate Christ" (I Cor. 11:1).

David made a sacrifice. Earlier he had said, "I will not offer burnt offerings to the Lord my God with that which costs me nothing" (II Sam. 24:24). David did not say, "Well, God, I am a very wealthy man. I'll give you out of my abundance. Here is a little token, a little tip. You know what the market has been lately. The elections are right around the corner. The economy is so unsettled. Interest rates are still quite questionable." No, David didn't say these things. He led by example. He gave a sacrificial gift out of his personal treasury.

As a pastor I wrestled with this. On the surface it appears to be that the Scripture is in contradiction. David specifically tells the people the amount of his personal gift, and yet I remember that Jesus said on the Sermon on the Mount that we should not let one hand know what our other hand is doing. There are many that are quick to point to these words of Jesus in the Sermon on the Mount. Is the Scripture in conflict? Was David out of line here? Let's note carefully the words Jesus preached on the grassy hillside in Galilee:

"Take heed that you do not do your charitable deeds before men, to be seen by them. Otherwise you have no reward from your Father in heaven. Therefore, when you do a charitable deed, do not sound a trumpet before you as the hypocrites do in the synagogues and in the streets, that they may have glory from men. Assuredly, I say to you, they have their reward. But when you do a charitable deed, do not let your left hand know what your right hand is doing, that your charitable deed may be in secret; and your Father who sees in secret will Himself reward you openly. And when you pray, you shall not be like the hypocrites. For they love to pray standing in the synagogues and on the corners of the streets, that they may be seen by men. Assuredly, I say to you, they have their reward. But you, when you pray, go into your room, and when you have shut your door, pray to your Father who is in the secret place; and your Father who sees in secret will reward you openly. And when you pray, do not use vain repetitions as the heathen do. For they think that they will be heard for their many words. Therefore do not be like them. For your Father knows the things you have need of before you ask Him" (Matt. 6:1-8).

Does Jesus mean that all giving is to be done in secret? If so, in the context, it must mean that all praying is to be done in secret. We know this is certainly not the case because as we read the Gospels we find the Lord Jesus praying publicly on almost every page and three times from the cross itself! The key to understanding this passage is to note the type of giving Jesus was discussing in the Sermon on the Mount. It was "giving to the needy." The King James Version translates it "alms." This was the specific type of giving which Jesus was referring to that should be done in secret. He was reacting to the custom of the blowing of the trumpets when a rich man would walk through the lines of poor beggars and toss in a few coins. The Lord Jesus was not referring to all giving here any more than he was referring to all praying being done in secret in the same context. What are we saying? David was right in doing what he did because his motives and his heart were pure.

David was setting the example for his people as a leader should do. When the people found out that he was committed, they gave willingly. That puts the pastor on the spot, doesn't it? When we led our churches in major giving programs our family prayed much about what we would do with our personal treasures. Like King David, we shared with our people what God led us to do. It is the price of leadership. And, we have never once been able to outgive Him. We have seen the truth and the proof of Luke 6:38 over and over again. It says, "Give, and it will be given to you: good measure, pressed down, shaken together, and running over will be put into your bosom. For with the same measure that you use, it will be measured back to you." Like David, we find great joy in giving. What is the order of our giving? The very word "leader" implies paving the way not just with time and talent, but also with treasure.

An interesting thing happens next. David did not simply give his testimony, sit down, and leave it at that. He challenged his people. He was not afraid to ask his people to join him in giving. As soon as he told them what he was going to do, he asked this question, "Who then is willing to consecrate himself this day to the Lord?" (I Chr. 29:5).

The result of David's challenge was overwhelming. The people gave "willingly." The Bible records, "Then the people rejoiced, for they had offered willingly, because with a loyal heart they had offered willingly to the Lord; and King David also rejoiced greatly" (I Chr. 29:9). They rejoiced at their leader's sacrifice and they rose to meet the challenge. The people of God always rise to meet a God-caused challenge!

It is important to note that David did not ask the others to do anything that he had not done himself. He led the way by example. He didn't say, "I'll leave it to the princes and people to come up with the necessary funds for the construction of the temple. I'll give my time and my talent but I'll let the rich people do the rest." No! David led by example. He said, "Now for the house of my God I have prepared with all my might" (I Chr. 29:2). Then he challenged the people, "Who then is willing to consecrate himself this day to the Lord?" (I Chr. 29:5). The first words of the very next verse speak volumes, "Then the leaders of the fathers' houses, leaders of the tribes of Israel, the captains of thousands and of hundreds, with the officers over the king's work, offered willingly" (I Chr. 29:6).

It is a probing question, "Who is willing to consecrate himself today to the Lord?" At least five critical questions arise out of this verse. WHO? This is the real probing question. Will you? WHAT? What is it that David is challenging the people to do? He is challenging them to consecrate themselves to God.

There is an important order to follow here. They were first to give themselves. Then they were to give of their treasure. This is the way the Macedonians gave and were commended for all posterity by the apostle Paul. He said of them, "That in a great trail of affliction the abundance of their joy and their deep poverty abounded in the riches of their liberality" (II Cor. 8:2). He went on to say, "He who gathered much had nothing left over, and he who gathered little had no lack" (II Cor. 8:15). HOW? This is another important question arising out of verse five. That is, how were they to give? The answer is "willingly." This was a call for voluntary, self-sacrificing service. Nothing is gained for the glory of God until our hearts are willing. WHEN? When were they to consecrate themselves to God? Today! The need is urgent! Today is not too early. Tomorrow may be too late. The time is now "for such a time as this." TO WHOM? The final question of verse five is an important one. To whom are we to give? Are we to give to the church? Are we to give to the new buildings? No! We are to give to the Lord! Here is our highest service produced by a noble motive. "Who is willing to consecrate himself today to the Lord? The people picked up the challenge of David and they gave "willingly." The Bible records, "I know also, my God, that You test the heart and have pleasure in uprightness. As for me, in the uprightness of my heart I have willingly offered all these things; and now with joy I have seen Your people, who are present here to offer willingly to you" (I Chr. 29:17). The offering received by the Israelites was a free will offering. No one told anyone else what to give. David did not tell the leaders or the people what to give. He did not assess anyone a certain amount. David simply told the people what he and his family were going to do and challenged them to meet God and do what God impressed upon their hearts. I have a word for this. I call it grace giving. There is a kind of giving which one might call "guilt giving." It says, "I will give because I ought to give." There is also "grudge giving." It says, "I will give because I have to give." But neither of these are seen in the fund raising program of the temple. What is seen here is what we desire. It is "grace giving" which says, "I will give willingly because I want to give."

When God's order for giving is carried out it results in great rejoicing. It is not surprising that those who have no real joy or rejoicing are usually those who are selfish and stingy. The Israelites were so full of joy one would think they must have just received some tremendous gift. After all, most people find joy in getting! But here we see an amazing principle. Their joy was from giving and not from getting. The world says joy comes from getting. We who know Christ know better. The Word says real joy comes from giving. David and his people discovered the truth that "it is more blessed to give than to receive" (Acts 20:35).

What was the outcome of it all? The giving became contagious. First David gave, then the leaders gave, then all Israel got in on it and gave willingly. David said, "Now with joy I have seen Your people, who are present here to offer willingly to you" (I Chr. 29:17).

The occasion of our giving is God-caused. The order of our giving is first the leader, then the leadership, then the people. I sense what was in David's heart when he said, "Nor will I offer burnt offerings to the Lord my God with that which costs me nothing" (II Sam. 24:24). My continual prayer is that it might be said of us what was said of the Israelites, "Then the people rejoiced, for they had offered willingly, because with a loyal heart they had offered willingly to the Lord; and King David also rejoiced greatly" (I Chr. 29:9).

Principle number three: The origin of our giving

 "...For all things come from You, and of Your own we have given You." I Chronicles 29:14

"But who am I, and who are my people, that we should be able to offer so willingly as this? For all things come from You, and of Your own we have given You. For we are aliens and pilgrims before You, as were all our fathers; our days on earth are as a shadow, and without hope. O Lord our God, all this abundance that we have prepared to build You a house for Your holy name is from Your hand, and is all Your own" (I Chr. 29:14-16).

Where do we find the origin of our giving? How can we possibly give what God has impressed upon our hearts? Where is the origin of our giving? Many are quick to look into the bank account balances. Others look to the origin of their giving in stock portfolios or life insurance policies or the like. What is the origin of our giving? David discovered it! He said, "For all things come from You, and of Your own we have given You" (I Chr. 29:14). This is what the songwriter meant when he said, "All I have needed Thy hand has provided; great is Thy faithfulness, Lord unto me."

As a pastor, I often felt in my own heart what David surely felt when he said, "Who am I, and who are my people, that we should be able to offer so willingly as this?" (I Chr. 29:14). How can this possibly come about? The secret is in the last phrase in verse 14. Listen to it. Don't miss it. Here is the key for our personal stewardship. "For all things come from You, and of Your own we have given You" (I Chr. 29:14).

Do you see it? Everything belongs to God. We are not to give out of our limited resources, but we are privileged to give out of God's unlimited resources. It all comes from God and we have the ability to "give out of God's hand." God owns all the wealth in this world and the next. David said it this way, "For all that is in heaven and in earth is Yours" (I Chr. 29:11). In the Psalms he declared, "The earth is the Lord's, and all its fullness" (Ps. 24:1). Paul put it this way, "For of Him and through Him and to Him are all things, to whom be glory forever" (Rom. 11:36). Yes, God owns all the wealth in this world and the next. Not only does God own everything, God wants his wealth in circulation. We learn this from the familiar passage from Malachi which said, "Bring all the tithes into the storehouse, that there may be food in My house, and try Me now in this, says the Lord of hosts, if I will not open for you the windows of heaven and pour out for you such blessing that there will not be room enough to receive it" (Mal. 3:10). In God's economy the earth had one theme in the beginning. It was give — give — give — give. The sun gave. The earth gave. The animals gave. Man gave. The trees gave. The enemy then introduced a new concept and it was get — get — get — get. And man became greedy and began to live by this philosophy. However, God wants his wealth in circulation.

Think this through. God owns it all and wants it in circulation. Here is another important point. All God's wealth belongs to His children. Listen to Paul, "And if children, then heirs — heirs of God and joint heirs with Christ, if indeed we suffer with Him, that we may also be glorified together" (Rom. 8:17). We are heirs of God. It all belongs to us. You say if we are heirs then where are our riches? How do we lay hold on what is ours from God? Now, if God owns it all, wants it in circulation, and it belongs to us…how do we get in on it? The way to appropriate God's wealth is to give. This is what Jesus is trying to get us to see when He said, "Give, and it will be given to you: good measure, pressed down, shaken together, and running over will be put into your bosom. For with the same measure that you use, it will be measured back to you" (Luke 6:38). We are to give out of God's resources, not our own. David put it this way, "Give out of God's hand." We are not necessarily to give what we think we can afford, but we are to reach over into His abundant and unlimited resources and give from them. What a privilege. The issue is not what do I have the ability to do. That philosophy is giving out of my own hand and God gets no glory in that. The issue is what has God said that He desires to do through me? What is it that He desires for me to believe by faith to give from His hand? What are we saying? Everything comes from God! He is the origin of our giving. David said it well when he said, "For all things come from You, and of Your own we have given You" (I Chr. 29:14).

Everything comes from God. This is what David is reminding his people when he says, "For we are aliens and pilgrims before You...our days on earth are as a shadow" (I Chr. 29:15). Life is short — too short. Our days are like a shadow. We only pass this way once. We are merely stewards along this journey. The question is, "What have you done with that which God has entrusted with you?" Some of my readers have no time to lose. Some of you have hair that is graying and may find this to be the last great opportunity in your entire lifetime to do something big for God.

The way is before us "for such a time as this". The occasion of our giving is God-caused. The order of our giving is first the heart and then the personal treasure. The origin of our giving is in God Himself. We are not to give from our own limited resources but out of His hand from His unlimited resources. "Everything comes from God."

Principle number four: The object of our giving

 "…with joy I have seen Your people, who are present here to offer willingly to You."
I Chronicles 29:17

"I know also, my God, that You test the heart and have pleasure in uprightness. As for me, in the uprightness of my heart I have willingly offered all these things; and now with joy I have seen Your people, who are present here to offer willingly to You" (I Chr. 29:17).

To what or to whom are we being challenged to give? Were the Israelites giving their personal treasures to the temple? Are we giving our personal treasures to the church? Are we giving our personal treasures to brick, or mortar, or buildings? What is the object of our giving? Note carefully what David says, "…with joy I have seen Your people, who are present here to offer willingly to You" (I Chr. 29:17).

One might say, "I thought they were giving to the temple." To whom were they giving? They were giving to God. They were not giving to the temple. To whom are we giving? What is the object of our giving? We are giving to God. We are not giving to new buildings or to our church. When we put a handle on this vital principle, it will be a breakthrough for us as it was for the Israelites. The object of our giving is the Lord Jesus Himself. We simply happen to be giving through our local churches to Him.

As much as I love my church, my family and I are not giving our personal treasures to the church. We are not giving one dime to concrete or steel or mortar or concrete block or tile or carpet or pews. The object of our giving is the Lord Himself. It just happens to be that we are giving to Him through a great soul-saving station. As we take from His hand, we put it back into His other hand. And He has a way of seeing that He can trust us and when He does, He gives, and gives, and gives again. The object of our giving is the Lord Himself!

Principle number five: The opportunity of our giving

 "...in the uprightness of my heart I have willingly offered all these things*..." I Chronicles 29:17-18*

"I know also, my God, that You test the heart and have pleasure in uprightness. As for me, in the uprightness of my heart I have willingly offered all these things; and now with joy I have seen Your people, who are present here to offer willingly to You. O Lord God of Abraham, Isaac, and Israel, our fathers, keep this forever in the intent of the thoughts of the heart of Your people, and fix their heart toward You" (I Chr. 29:17-18).

How does a Christian walk in "uprightness?" He does so by doing what he claims to be. A Christian walks in integrity when his walk matches his talk and when his life matches his lips. We say we are a people of faith. We say we live by faith. David reminds us that "God tests the heart and has pleasure in uprightness" (I Chr. 29:17). Yes, God tests our hearts to see if we really dare to live by faith. The Bible admonishes us, "As you therefore have received Christ Jesus the Lord, so walk in Him" (Col. 2:6). Many are quick to say we are saved by faith.

But so few of us continue in the same way. We say we are saved by faith, but we live our life by works. If faith is good enough to save us it is surely good enough to live by. So many Christians who walk through the door of Christ by faith revert to what they can see and do themselves in living the Christian life. God is testing the integrity of our hearts.

What is the opportunity of our giving? The opportunity before us is to please God by living by faith. He is "pleased with integrity." Some of us pride ourselves in our own integrity and need to hear these words and heed them. We say that we are a Christian by faith alone in Jesus Christ. We say we believe God will never leave us. We say we believe all of His promises. And yet so many of us live by sight. Our hope is in our savings accounts or stock portfolios or real estate holdings or retirement packages. This is a call for integrity in Christian living. David put it this way, "I know also, my God, that You test the heart and have pleasure in uprightness" (I Chr. 29:17). What an opportunity is ours to say to the world, "All things are possible — only believe!"

Now, this creates a great deal of pressure upon an individual. However, the pressure is put upon us by the Holy Spirit Himself. When we gave to build the new buildings in Fort Lauderdale we made a faith pledge to God that was given weekly and systematically over three years. Many of us have spent a lifetime doing that with the world. We have done such things as sign thirty-year mortgages with a lending institution and promise to pay on the first of the month for the next thirty years.

Is there a Biblical basis for a faith pledge? Indeed there is. Do you remember when Paul wrote to the church at Corinth and challenged them to make a gift? Listen to his own words, "Now concerning the collection for the saints, as I have given orders to the churches of Galatia, so you must do also: On the first day of the week let each one of you lay something aside, storing up as he may prosper, that there be no collections when I come. And when I come, whomever you approve by your letters I will send to bear your gift to Jerusalem. But if it is fitting that I go also, they will go with me" (I Cor. 16:1-4).

One year later Paul writes back to the same church (recorded in II Corinthians, Eight and Nine) and says to them that he is sending Titus to make sure the gift is ready when he gets there. Note carefully what Paul says, "So let each one give as he purposes in his heart, not grudgingly or of necessity; for God loves a cheerful giver" (II Cor. 9:7). The New International Version translates that Scripture "That which you decided in your heart to give." In the original language the word is "prohaireomai." It means "to decide ahead of time to do a certain thing." The Corinthians had made a faith-pledge ahead of time and they gave it when the time came.

We did exactly the same thing Paul admonished this first century church to do. We decided ahead of time what we were going to give from God's hand to the Lord over the next three years. We were challenged to make a gift just as Paul challenged the church in I Corinthians Chapter 16. Over the next three years we gave what we decided "ahead of time" to give.

We called it a faith-pledge. It doesn't really matter what you call it as long as you meet God and give from His hand.

We are now at the heart of the issue before us. We are dealing with God Himself who knows our hearts. In a very real sense our own spiritual integrity is revealed at this point. It is no wonder some feel pressure from the Holy Spirit. We call it a faith pledge because the issue is our faith in God's ability to provide. The issue is not our faith in what the economy is going to do or who the next president of United States will be, nor anything else that man can do, manipulate, or orchestrate. The opportunity before us is our faith to believe in God's readiness and willingness to provide through us from His hand for His work. What an opportunity! We have the opportunity in our giving to show the world that Jesus Christ is alive and at work in and through us to the Father's glory.

Our integrity and our motives are at issue here. Do you know that it is possible for a Christian to do something that in the eyes of man is wonderful but in the eyes of God is detestable? There are a lot of folks who do things in the eyes of men that are wonderful. Some even receive plaques and the like for them, but Jesus put it this way, "No one can serve two masters; for either he will hate the one and love the other, or else he will be loyal to the one and despise the other. You cannot serve God and mammon" (Matt. 6:24). Now the Pharisees, who were lovers of money, also heard all these things, and they derided Him. And He said to them, "You are those who justify yourselves before men, but God knows your hearts. For what is highly esteemed among men is an abomination in the sight of God" (Luke 16:13-15). David said the same thing in the following way, "I know also, my God, that You test the heart and have pleasure in uprightness. As for me, in the uprightness of my heart I have willingly offered all these things; and now with joy I have seen Your people, who are present here to offer willingly to You" (I Chr. 29:17).

As commendable as David's efforts were and as valuable as his gifts were, had his motives been the applause of men the whole matter would have been an abomination to God and detestable before His eyes. David sought to walk by faith in integrity and to glorify God in the process. We catch a glimpse of his heart when he says, "O Lord God of Abraham, Isaac, and Israel, our fathers, keep this forever in the intent of the thoughts of the heart of Your people, and fix their heart toward You" (I Chr. 29:18). David desired for it to become a lifestyle, not only for himself, but for his people. It will become a lifestyle for us as we keep our hearts loyal to Him. David's concern was that his people continue and that his pattern of giving not just become a one-time shot, but a transformation of a lifestyle toward faith and dependence upon God forever.

Our personal giving is the place where our spiritual integrity is revealed before God. God is measuring our personal integrity. David said the task was great because the temple was "not for man but for the Lord God" (I Chr. 29:1). May it be said of us what was said of the church at Rome, "I thank my God through Jesus Christ for you all, that your faith is spoken of throughout the whole world" (Rom. 1:8). What an opportunity we have to be a blessing and encouragement to the work of God around the world.

Principle number six: The objective of our giving

 "...so all the assembly blessed the Lord God..."
I Chronicles 29:20

"But who am I, and who are my people, that we should be able to offer so willingly as this? For all things come from You, and of Your own we have given You" (I Chr. 29:14).

"I know also, my God, that You test the heart and have pleasure in uprightness. As for me, in the uprightness of my heart I have willingly offered all these things; and now with joy I have seen Your people, who are present here to offer willingly to You" (I Chr. 29:17).

"Then David said to all the assembly, "Now bless the Lord Your God." So all the assembly blessed the Lord God of their fathers, and bowed their heads and prostrated themselves before the Lord and the king" (I Chr. 29:20)

What is the objective in giving? Our objective is that everyone become involved. Our objective is that everyone prays and everyone fasts and everyone meets God and everyone gives from God's hand. The Israelites victory won the day because each one did his or her part. The one thing that stands out in each of the above passages of Scripture from Chronicles is that each one of the Israelites was involved. It was a case of total participation.

The early church had the same objective and followed the Israelites example. "When the Day of Pentecost had fully come, they were all with one accord in one place" (Acts 2:1). "Now all who believed were together, and had all things in common, and sold their possessions and goods, and divided them among all, as anyone had need" (Acts 2:44-45). "Now the multitude of those who believed were of one heart and one soul; neither did anyone say that any of the things he possessed was his own, but they had all things in common. And with great power the apostles gave witness to the resurrection of the Lord Jesus. And great grace was upon them all. Nor was there anyone among them who lacked; for all who were possessors of lands or houses sold them, and brought the proceeds of the things that were sold, and laid them at the apostles' feet; and they distributed to each as anyone had need" (Acts 4:32-35).

Our objective in giving is the same. We long to see everyone involved with no one missing the blessing of giving. Someone might say, "I have no money; I have nothing to give." Then give from God's hand. Proverbs 13:23 reminds us, "Much food is in the fallow ground of the poor." Fallow ground is ground that has not been used, plowed, nor planted for a considerable period of time. God is saying there are resources available where we think there are none. There is much food in the fallow ground of the poor! God show us fallow ground!

Everyone gave to the Lord for the building of the temple.

Old men gave. Young men gave. Middle age men gave. Women gave. Young couples gave. Singles gave. Teenagers and boys and girls gave. Those without money sold their possessions and gave them. It was victory day because everyone got in on it.

Remember, the occasion of our offering is God-caused. The order of our offering is first from the heart and then from our gifts. The origin of our offering is to give from God's hand. The object of our offering is the Lord Himself. The opportunity of our offering is to please God by being people of faith. The objective is everyone being involved.

Principle number seven: The outcome of our giving

 "...Yours, O Lord, is the greatness, the power and the glory, the victory and the majesty..."
I Chronicles 29:10-13

"Therefore David blessed the Lord before all the assembly; and David said: "Blessed are You, Lord God of Israel, our Father, forever and ever. Yours, O Lord, is the greatness, the power and the glory, the victory and the majesty; for all that is in heaven and in earth is Yours; Yours is the kingdom, O Lord, and You are exalted as head over all. Both riches and honor come from You, and You reign over all. In Your hand is power and might; in Your hand it is to make great and to give strength to all. Now therefore, our God, we thank you and praise Your glorious name" (I Chr. 29:10-13).

"'I know also, my God, that You test the heart and have

pleasure in uprightness. As for me, in the uprightness of my heart I have willingly offered all these things; and now with joy I have seen Your people, who are present here to offer willingly to You. O Lord God of Abraham, Isaac, and Israel, our fathers, keep this forever in the intent of the thoughts of the heart of Your people, and fix their heart toward You. And give my son Solomon a loyal heart to keep Your commandments and Your testimonies and Your statutes, to do all these things, and to build the temple for which I have made provision.' Then David said to all the assembly, 'Now bless the Lord your God.' So all the assembly blessed the Lord God of their fathers, and bowed their heads and prostrated themselves before the Lord and the king" (I Chr. 29:17-20).

What was the outcome of the Israelites giving? God got the glory! The people pointed to His greatness and not that of David or the leadership. The outcome of their giving was all praise going to the Lord God. Can you imagine their joy when the offering was taken? Can you just see David standing up in front of his people saying "Blessed are You, Lord God of Israel, our Father, forever and ever. Yours, O Lord, is the greatness, the power and the glory, the victory and the majesty; for all that is in heaven and in earth is Yours; Yours is the kingdom, O Lord, and You are exalted as head over all. Both riches and honor come from You, and You reign over all. In Your hand is power and might; In Your hand it is to make great and to give strength to all. Now therefore, our God, we thank You and praise Your glorious name" (I Chr. 29:10-13). God was glorified that day because where a man puts his treasure his heart is sure to follow. They "bowed their heads and prostrated themselves before the Lord and the king" (I Chr. 29:20).

Their giving resulted in revival. Why is this? So often greed is one of the major obstacles to revival. Usually, in the end, money is the last thing to which people hold. There are a lot of people who give their time. There are a lot of people who give their talents but so many hold back their personal treasures. These men and women said, "God it's all yours; here it is!" And Jesus said, "For where your treasure is, there your heart will be also" (Matt. 6:21). Our hearts always follow our treasures. If we primarily put our treasures in some kind of activity, our hearts will be there. If we put our treasures in the work of God, our hearts will be there. And revival will result! The Israelites made a sacrifice for those who would come after them. They gave to the Lord God…for others and not for themselves.

One might think that such incredible success as David and his people saw would make them burst with pride. Quite the contrary, it brought a deep sense of gratitude and a humble spirit. "David said to the whole assembly . . .'Look what we have done!'" No! That's not what he said. He said, "Now bless the Lord your God. So all the assembly blessed the Lord God of their fathers, and bowed their heads and prostrated themselves before the Lord and the king" (I Chr. 29:20). What an outcome there was of praise and worship. Oh that we might join them in bringing great honor and glory to the living Christ "for such a time as this."

The task before the 21st century church is great. We are a part of something grand and glorious because what we are about is "not for man but for the Lord God." How can we do it? We can follow the example of the Israelites and these scriptural guidelines for supernatural giving:

(1) *The occasion of our giving.* The occasion of our giving is God-caused. Ours is a God-caused need. Remember, if God's former blessings brought about our present needs, his future blessings will be sufficient to meet the needs the former blessings have caused! We can trust the Lord. He is the initiator of our need.

(2) *The order of our giving.* The pastor and leadership must lead the way and the people will follow. First we are to give ourselves and then our gifts. May we be able to join the Israelites and may it be said of us, "The people rejoiced, for they had offered willingly, because with a loyal heart they had offered willingly to the Lord; and King David also rejoiced greatly" (I Chr. 29:9).

(3) *The origin of our giving.* Our ability to give comes from God. "Everything comes from God and we have given only what comes from His hand." He owns it all, wants his wealth in circulation. We are his heirs, and the way to appropriate his wealth is to give! He is the origin of our giving.

(4) *The object of our giving.* We are not giving to brick, nor mortar, nor our church, but the object of our giving is to the Lord Himself. David put it this way, "Now with joy I have seen Your people, who are present here to offer willingly to You" (I Chr. 29:17).

(5) *The opportunity of our giving.* We have the opportunity to be a tremendous witness for Christ by walking by faith. God knows our hearts. Integrity is the by-word. We say we are a people of faith and now it is time to let our walk match our talk and our life match our lips. Like David, we too know that God "tests the heart and has pleasure in uprightness" (I Chr. 29:17).

(6) *The objective of our giving.* The objective of our giving is that everyone meet God and give by revelation. Everyone being involved is the key to victory. No one is unimportant. Remember there is much food in the fallow ground of the poor.

(7) *The outcome of our giving.* The ultimate outcome of it all is that the Lord Jesus Christ might be glorified and honored and praised. Our desire is that we praise the Lord our God and give Him glory through the whole experience.

Yes, *money talks…but what is it really saying?*